He Led Me

Alex and Elizabeth Maclennan on their wedding day
Photo: Free Presbyterian Church Archive

He Led Me

Autobiography, diaries
and meditations
of Alex Maclennan

Edited by

Norman Campbell and Robert Dickie

REFORMATION PRESS
2018

British Library Cataloguing-in-Publication Data
A catalogue record for this book is available from
the British Library

PAPERBACK EDITION
ISBN 978-1-872556-36-9

© Reformation Press 2018

Published by
Reformation Press, 11 Churchill Drive, Stornoway
Isle of Lewis, Scotland HS1 2NP

www.reformationpress.co.uk

Printed by www.lulu.com

Also available as a Kindle e-book
ISBN 978-1-872556-37-6

Contents

Preface

THE survival of Alex Maclennan's writings is due largely to two people. His widow Elizabeth kept them after his death and gave many of the papers, including most of his diaries, to Mrs Lilian Campbell (née Fraser). Mrs Maclennan wished them to be published. Mrs Campbell carefully preserved them for a number of years. The material is now in the care of the Free Presbyterian Church of Scotland's Archive Committee.

The diaries published here cover the years from 1957 to 1960 and from 1966 to 1970.[1] Other diaries are extant but it has not been possible to access them.

Alex Maclennan kept these diaries with a view to others reading them in the future. A number of entries confirm this. For example, one entry reads: 'Signed: AML. Anyone finding this diary may read it, hope you may find some interesting sentiments.' Furthermore, he occasionally directly addressed future potential readers of the diaries. A typical example is in the entry of 31st December 1968, where he summed up his

---

[1] The 1956 diary is also available, but the contents are significantly different from the present series. Alex Maclennan's stated aim that year was to write in the style of the Daily Thoughts genre of Christian literature. This may be published in future. Alex wrote only a handful of entries in his 1958 diary; two have been included for their usefulness.

present spiritual exercise and continued: 'So, my dear friends, I may never pass this way again. I am on the border of the eternal world, in my 80th year. May we meet in the better country. Good night.'

Alex's service to the cause of Christ was intertwined with that of his minister, Rev. Donald Alexander Macfarlane (1889–1979). Mr Macfarlane became minister of the Dingwall and Beauly congregations in 1930[2] and retired from that pastorate in 1973.[3] Alex's work as a missionary increased as he and other elders, including his brother John Maclennan,[4] conducted public worship when Mr Macfarlane was unable to do so due to ill health. The explanation of the Bible text given by elders or other male communicants on such occasions is more usually described as 'exhorting' than 'preaching' in the Free

---

[2] Previous to this, Mr Macfarlane had served in the joint charge of Lairg, Bonar, Dornoch and Rogart (1914–1921) and in Oban (1921–1930). He was a much loved preacher, a tutor of divinity students in Greek and Hebrew, respected for his intellectual abilities, and known for his kindness. His first wife was Catherine Cameron from Oban; she died in 1955. His married his second wife, Ella Finlayson, in 1957. She outlived him by many years, passing away in 2015. See John Tallach, *I Shall Arise: The life and ministry of Donald A. Macfarlane* (Aberdeen: Faro Publishing, 1984).

[3] The manse for the combined pastoral charge is in Dingwall.

[4] Alex's brother John worked on railway track maintenance near Muir of Ord. John was highly regarded for his godliness but was not so gifted as a public speaker. He died in January 1979, at the age of eighty-seven. He was remembered as a quiet, gentle and humble person who knew how to encourage young believers. The Synod tribute for John said: 'His humble, gracious and loving spirit endeared him to all who knew him.' 'Synod Tribute to the late Mr John Maclennan, Elder, Beauly', *Free Presbyterian Church of Scotland, Proceedings of Synod* [hereafter cited as *Synod Proceedings*], *May, 1979* (Glasgow, 1979), p. 104.

Presbyterian Church although Alex did use the latter term at times.

Alex was circumspect in what he recorded in his diary: rare references to sensitive church business and controversy have been removed. The entries published here were selected for spiritual and historical interest. The names of hospital patients and those professing faith for the first time have been removed or anonymised to respect their and their families' privacy. Minor editorial changes have been made where appropriate, including changes to punctuation and layout.

Footnotes have been provided to explain words, expressions or locations with which some readers may not be familiar, to quote Bible texts cited in the diaries, and (where possible) to provide further information about most of the people mentioned in the book. Information referenced from the *Free Presbyterian Magazine* and from recent *Proceedings of Synod* is mostly available on the Free Presbyterian Church's website (www.fpchurch.org) and readers are encouraged to read the full articles.

The publisher wishes to thank Lilian Campbell, the Free Presbyterian Church of Scotland Archives Committee, and its convenor Rev. Dr Douglas Somerset, for supporting the publication of the diaries. In addition. the publisher acknowledges the kindness of Alasdair and Morag MacDonald (Kiltarlity) in providing most of the notes of Alex's addresses when he took church services. Thanks are also due to another friend (who wishes to remain anonymous), who often heard Alex, for the notes of his New Year's Day address on Psalm 100.

Much useful support and background information was provided by a large number of people. The publisher wishes to acknowledge his debt to them, particularly Donella Campbell (Stornoway), John Campbell (Inverness), Mairi Campbell (Ullapool), Roderick Campbell (Glendale), Donald and Margaret Fraser (Daviot), John and Mairi Fraser (Inverness), the late Edward Greene (Oxford), George Harvey (Inverness), Morag Hymers (Edinburgh), Iain and Joan Livingstone (Beauly), Rev. George Macaskill (Stornoway), Rev. Calum MacInnes and Catherine MacInnes (Inverness), Ally Maclean (Dingwall), Murdo MacLean (Glasgow), Rev. John MacLeod (London), Rev. Kenneth Macleod (Inverness), Tom Maton (Gairloch), Roy Middleton (Barnoldswick), Rev. Donald Ross (Laide), Edward Ross (Lochcarron), Rev. Neil Ross (Dingwall), and Rev. John Tallach (Inverness). The publisher is also grateful to James Dickie (Inverness), who designed the book cover.

Elizabeth Maclennan repeatedly expressed her wish that the writings of her late husband should be preserved and published. The publisher is confident that these diary excerpts and notes of addresses will be profitable to many readers.

STORNOWAY
NOVEMBER 2018

Introductory sketch

A LEX MACLENNAN was born on 9th September 1889. He grew up on the island of Rona off the north coast of Raasay near Skye. The small island had largely been served by missionaries,[5] parents taking their children to Raasay for baptism.[6] Alex's father Alexander was from Kishorn, his mother Mary was from Gairloch, Wester Ross, and Alex was the sixth of their eight children.[7]

The Rona people had always been part of the Raasay congregation, who had only gained their first stated Free Church minister in 1851 in the person of William S. MacDougall.[8]

---

[5] A home missionary in Scotland is a man paid a salary to take services and carry out pastoral visitation, normally in one specific congregation, but who is not ordained as a minister. The post has become relatively rare in recent decades.

[6] Charles Macleod, *South Rona: The island and its people*, ed. Rebecca Mackay, (Raasay: Raasay Heritage Trust, 2016), p. 20. This Rona is not to be confused with its more northerly namesake, some 41 miles (66 km) north-north-east of the Isle of Lewis.

[7] In order of birth, the children were: Jessie, Margaret, John, Kenneth, May, Alexander, John and Mary.

[8] Mr MacDougall (1814–1892) was born in Downpatrick, County Down. He was of Argyll stock and the family moved to farm in Kintyre when he was ten years old. After Raasay, he was a minister of Appin in Argyllshire, and then Fodderty in Ross-shire. He was an ally of Rev. Dr John Kennedy of Dingwall, describing him in his diary as 'my beloved friend and nearest brother-minister'. An obitu-

Alex's father, Alexander Maclennan, had been appointed missionary in 1884.[9] In a newspaper article in later years, Alex recalled a trip to the now-deserted isle of Rona.[10] Visiting the old church that summer, he said that it could seat a hundred people and that people would come to services in summer from small nearby communities and even from the Applecross coast to the east across the Inner Sound.[11] As a young man he had to sit on the pulpit steps on such days, that being the only space available.[12]

A flavour of the godliness to be found in Rona can be seen in the case of John Maclennan (known as Iain Òg—'Young' John in Gaelic) who was a respected old man on the island.[13] On the Sabbaths that the stated missionary was away at Kyle Rona,[14] Iain Òg would hold a meeting in his house. A teacher on the island commented, 'He [...] engaged in prayer and, if his exposition was remarkable, his prayer may be described as

---

ary for Mr MacDougall recorded: 'His preaching was remarkable, not only for its scripturalness, but for clearness, simplicity, order, tenderness, and unction.' 'Rev. William S. McDougall, Fodderty', *The Free Church of Scotland Monthly Record* [hereafter cited as *Monthly Record*] (December 1892): p. 301.

[9] Macleod, *South Rona*, p. 19.

[10] The last indigenous family left in 1944. The manned lighthouse was automated in 1977, leaving only a few staff at the Admiralty/BUTEC (British Underwater Test and Evaluation Centre) military test and evaluation range.

[11] Rona lies approximately 4 miles (under 7 km) west of the Applecross peninsula.

[12] *Ross-shire Journal*, 18th December 1953, republished in Macleod, *South Rona*, p. 52.

[13] Macleod, *South Rona*, p. 60. Mr Macleod reprinted an article by James Nicolson of Braes: 'Recollections of Iain Òg, Rona', *Free Presbyterian Magazine* [hereafter cited as *FPM*] Vol. 46 (July 1941): pp. 68–72.

[14] A village on the far northern tip of Raasay.

wonderful. He gave the impression that he was unconscious of anyone listening to him but the Invisible One.'[15] Iain Òg was noted for his generosity, as well as for a solemn warning he gave when an old man and his family were complicit in half of the grazings being taken away from one of the townships on the island. The warning Iain Òg gave as to the dire consequences was fulfilled.[16]

Another example of the spirituality in Rona is to be seen in the obituary for Donald MacLeod, elder in Raasay. It was said of him, 'He was often at private prayer and, like some others of the Lord's people, left the marks of his knees on the hills and rocks of the island of Rona, pouring out his complaints before the Lord.'[17]

Almost all the Rona people and most of the Raasay people separated from the Free Church with their minister Rev. Donald Macfarlane[18] in 1893.[19] Alex Maclennan's father, Alexander, had nailed his colours to the mast on the Monday of the June 1893 communion in Raasay, when the people expressed their support for Rev. Macfarlane in separating from the Free Church. The minister had tabled a protest at the General Assembly that year as the constitution of the church had been changed by legislation called the Declaratory Act, which

---

[15] Macleod, *South Rona*, p. 60.

[16] Macleod, *South Rona*, p. 61.

[17] 'Donald Macleod, Elder, Raasay', *FPM* Vol. 38, (March 1934): pp. 464–466. He died in 1933.

[18] Rev. Donald Macfarlane (1834–1926) was minister in Strathconon, Moy (Inverness-shire), Kilmallie, and Raasay Free Church congregations. After separating in 1893 he remained as the Free Presbyterian minister of Raasay until called to Dingwall in 1903, where he served until his death. Donald Beaton, *Memoir, Diary & Remains of the Rev. Donald Macfarlane, Dingwall*, (Inverness: n.p., 1929).

[19] Macleod, *South Rona*, p. 20.

allowed heresy. Alexander had compared the Declaratory Act to cholera. He was known to be a great admirer of Dr Kennedy[20] and Rev. Alexander MacColl.[21] His obituarist, Rev. Neil Cameron,[22] commented on his grasp of language, mental abilities and preaching style: 'He made good use of

---

[20] John Kennedy (1819–1884) was a son of Rev. John Kennedy, Killearnan (1772–1841). He was the minister of Dingwall Free Church from 1844 until his death. An influential doctrinal and experimental preacher, he strongly promoted the Reformed faith, and opposed the American revivalists Dwight L. Moody (1837–1899) and Ira D. Sankey (1840–1908) who visited the Highlands in summer 1874. He was given an honorary doctorate by Aberdeen University in 1873. Among his publications were *The Days of the Fathers in Ross-shire* (1861), and his biography of the Rev. John MacDonald of Ferintosh, *The Apostle of the North* (1866). Both have run to several editions.

[21] Alexander MacColl (1815–1889) was a powerful preacher of the gospel in the Free Church of Scotland. He lost his job as a teacher in Uig, Lewis at the Disruption of 1843. After serving as a missionary-minister in Lochcarron and Applecross from 1844, he was inducted to Duirinish in Skye in 1852, preaching there until 1870. His two later ministries were in Fort Augustus and Glen Moriston (1870–1877), then Lochalsh. He campaigned against the church union movement of 1863–1873, and against the Disestablishment movement. 'Rev. Alexander MacColl', *Monthly Record* (April 1889): p. 118.

[22] Rev. Neil Cameron (1854–1932) was born in Kilninver near Oban. He was educated in Kilchoan Public School, Ardnamurchan, and then in Onich in Lochaber. He helped rally the people to support the Free Presbyterian separation of 1893. After divinity training he served as minister of the St Jude's (Glasgow) congregation from 1896 until 1932. The foremost minister of the Church for most of his ministry, he wrote scores of obituaries in the early decades of the Church's existence.

illustrations in his public addresses, whereby he fixed what he meant an audience to grasp, indelibly on their memories.'[23]

The separation to defend the Bible and *Westminster Confession of Faith* brought its own measure of persecution in some places. It appears that Alex's father and the Rona community shared in that. A newspaper reported: 'It appears that Mr Maclennan, missionary at Rona, and Mr Mackenzie, missionary at Gairloch, have both received notice from the West Coast Mission[24] that their services are to be dispensed with. "Such proceedings on the part of this Mission is", adds a correspondent, "causing great surprise, as it professes to be neutral; but it is believed that those who are persecuting these men for leaving the Free Church have demanded their dismissal. One of the complaints against Mr Maclennan, Rona, is that he is making a division in the congregation; but there is only one solitary person in Rona who has not joined Mr Macfarlane, and he is not a native."'[25]

Alex's childhood memories included visits to Rona by Rev. Donald Macfarlane. Decades later (on Tuesday September 9th, 1969) Alex found an old couple reading the Bible at 5pm. He recorded in his diary:

> The chapter that was being read was that which contains the profound passage, 'Great is the mystery of godliness: God was manifest in the flesh.' I remember in my childhood days Rev. Donald Macfarlane being in our house in Rona at family worship and taking that chapter. That particular verse has re-

---

[23] 'The late Alexander MacLennan, Rona, Raasay', *FPM* Vol. 25 (January 1921): pp. 268–271.

[24] The interdenominational body was set up in 1855, providing missionaries and occasionally nurses for very remote communities. It was wound up in 1950.

[25] *Northern Chronicle*, 13th June 1894, p. 7.

mained in my mind ever since, about seventy years. There is no more weighty passage in Holy Writ.[26]

Before he left Rona, the looming Great War had begun to cast its shadows on even that remote community. Its approach remained a vivid memory. On Saturday 26th April 1969, he noted:

> I was up at John's this evening.[27] We read Luke 20 and 21 which are solemn indeed, ending with the admonition to be always ready for the coming of the Lord at death and the Judgment Day. Indeed the above were the last words my father read before I left home prior to the outbreak of World War One. He seemed to have an intimation that the judgments were coming. A man told me that Father preached a solemn sermon in Rona from Jeremiah, in which he took the portion 'Even the carcasses of men shall fall as dung upon the open field' before the Great War of 1914 broke out. The last words I heard him read were: 'What I say unto you, I say unto all, Watch.' Mark 13:37.

Alex left Rona for Australia in 1914, working in the Merchant Navy there and in New Zealand and Fiji. The long initial sea journey from Britain was to be a point of reference as Alex grew older and saw international travel become more convenient. In 1956 he noted:

---

[26] The incident may have taken place during Mr Macfarlane's visit to Rona in October 1900. See Donald Beaton, *Memoir, Diary & Remains of the Rev. Donald Macfarlane, Dingwall* (Inverness: Northern Counties Newspaper and Printing and Publishing Company, Limited, 1929), p. 90.

[27] The younger of two of Alex's siblings with the same name, this John lived very near to Alex in Muir of Ord.

I went in the early forenoon to Kiltarlity to see Iain Maciver who arrived recently from New Zealand by air. He left Christchurch, New Zealand on Friday and arrived London 3pm on Monday. When I went to Australasia in early 1914 we made a non-stop voyage. From the time we started off from Royal Albert Docks, London, the vessel's engines did not stop until we dropped anchor at Melbourne. Thirty-eight days of open sea, all the land we saw in that space was a glimpse of the Canaries and a barren island of grey rock in the middle of the Great Southern Ocean. My friend flew in three days.[28]

Alex's ship, the SS Muritai
Photo: Free Presbyterian Church Archive

Diaries he wrote while in the Merchant Navy show that Alex had a respect for the Sabbath and was aware of the efforts of others to keep it. During his Fiji voyage he wrote on a Saturday in August 1918: 'The natives are stowing the sugar as fast as they can, trying to get finished (I take it) before mid-

---

[28] Diary, Wednesday 11th April 1956.

night. They are very much averse to working on Sundays [*sic*], which I think is a remarkable fact. It shows that the missionaries sent there are doing splendid work.'[29] While in Gisborne, New Zealand, on the Sabbath afternoon, he would climb a hill next to the harbour to get away from the Sabbath-breaking on the ship and read his Bible.

Alex Maclennan as a young man[30]
Photo: Free Presbyterian Church Archive

---

[29] The date was 31st August 1918. During the voyage in the Pacific a 'strict lookout' was kept for floating mines which the Imperial German cruiser *SMS Wolf* was supposed to have laid. Alex Maclennan, *A Trip to the Fijis*; manuscript jotter, kindly loaned by Alasdair MacDonald, Kiltarlity.

[30] Alex sent this photo from Fiji, mounted on a stamped card. He subsequently printed on the card: 'Oh that I had a few of my years back again, with the added experience of age.'

Alex believed that he was called gradually by grace after he 'spent about twenty-three years of my life like a wild ass's colt on the mountains of vanity'. This places the beginning of his conversion in the time before leaving Rona for the Antipodes. He described it in the following words:

> It was a gradual protracted work by the Word and the Spirit of God. [...] Someone said that 'all on the way to heaven must pass Sinai and Calvary, though all do not get the same distinct view of them'. I cannot speak of the terrors of Sinai, nor do I consider that experience necessary to salvation. I can only say that I felt an extraordinary measure of the drawing power of God's everlasting love and great meltings of soul in secret prayer. [...] I can still remember the prayer my mother taught me when going to bed at four years of age: 'Dèan tròcair orm-sa a tha am pheacach, agus glan mi ann am fuil Chrìosda.'[31] I cannot get a better one to this day. I feel my profound need of it.

Alex returned home after the war. A time of blessing which he experienced on Rona in 1920 was described many years later. Writing to his sister, he described a trip there the day before:

> I then went up to the Faing Mhòr.[32] I prayed there and thanked the Lord [...] for the meltings of soul I experienced in that spot forty-five years ago which I can never forget, and would like one of these days back again. However, a better

---

[31] Gaelic: 'Have mercy on me a sinner, and cleanse me in the blood of Christ.'
[32] Gaelic: the big fank (sheepfold).

indication of my state is that Christ is becoming more glorious and precious in my eyes.[33]

He and his siblings and mother soon joined the mass exodus from the island. Jobs were almost non-existent and the crofts too small to be viable. They moved to the mainland after Alexander's death in 1920.[34] They were assigned a new smallholding in the Tomich district of Muir of Ord. It had been part of a large farm owned by the Lovat Estates.[35] The holding had no water supply until a water source was dug for Alex as part of a deal in which he sold some land to the businessman William Logan, founder of the airline which bears his name. The Logan purchase of part of Alex's 45-acre smallholding took place in 1950.[36]

Beauly church life

The Maclennan family worshipped in Beauly Free Presbyterian Church at Kilmorack.[37] Alex was to be closely involved in the work of the congregation for all his life.

---

[33] Letter dated 6th May 1965 to his sister May Dougan who lived in Tain, written from Arnish, Raasay.

[34] Macleod, *South Rona*, p. 65.

[35] The background is described in *The Braes, Parish of Kilmorack*, compiled by H.W. Harrison, (Beauly: Kilmorack Heritage Association, 2002), p. 203.

[36] William Logan (1913–1966) was a Dingwall-based civil engineer and Highland businessman who founded the Loganair airline. His construction company built many bridges, including the Tay Road Bridge, and hydroelectric projects. Logan was a Free Church man brought up in Muir of Ord, who would not allow Sabbath work by his staff. He was killed tragically when an air taxi he had hired privately crashed into Dunain Hill (Craig Dunain) just outside Inverness.

[37] Kilmorack is the name of the parish, Beauly the main village, and Balblair the actual site of the church building referred to here. Alex

A key figure in the formation of the Beauly congregation was Alexander Fraser (1818–1901). He had acted as an elder for almost fifty years, first in the Free Church and then in the Free Presbyterian Church. His obituary said: 'Since the formation of a Free Presbyterian congregation at Beauly he had rendered most valuable service—indeed, on him more than on any other single individual, responsibility in this rested.' Mr Fraser worked as a miller at nearby Belladrum[38] and had then become a merchant. His spiritual circle in Beauly included Thomas Fraser, Simon Campbell, Angus MacDonald (Urray), John Rose (latterly of Moy), John Campbell of Knockbain and others. The ministries of Rev. Archibald Cook,[39] Dr Mackay[40] and Dr Kennedy were of value to him.[41]

---

used Kilmorack and Beauly interchangeably for the name of the congregation.

[38] Belladrum is a farm and estate near Kiltarlity.

[39] Archie Cook (1775–1865) was an outstanding experience-focused preacher. Born on the Isle of Arran, he was missionary-minister in Bruan-Berriedale (Caithness) from 1822 until 1837. He became minister of the newly-formed North Church in Inverness in 1837 and took it into the Free Church in 1843. From 1844 until his death he served as pastor in Daviot Free Church. Norman Campbell, *One of Heaven's Jewels: Rev. Archibald Cook of Daviot and the (Free) North Church, Inverness* (Stornoway: Norman Campbell, 2009); *Eternal Reality: Sermons by Archibald Cook* (Glasgow: Free Presbyterian Publications, 2015).

[40] George Mackay (1796–1886) served as Established Church minister in Clyne (Sutherland) from 1828 until 1843, joined the Free Church, and was translated to the Free North Church, Inverness, in 1845, where he was minister until his death. He was awarded the degree of Doctor in Divinity (D.D.) by the University of Aberdeen in 1878. Hew Scott, *Fasti Ecclesiae Scoticanae: The Succession of Ministers in the Church of Scotland from the Reformation, Vol. VII* (Edinburgh: Oliver and Scott, 1928), p. 81.

[41] 'A brief Notice of the late Mr Alexander Fraser, Merchant, Beauly', *FPM* Vol. 6 (May 1901): pp. 30–32.

J. MacAulay was noted as missionary in 1907[42] but the supply arrangements for 1908 and 1909 are unclear. A divinity student provided supply from 1910 until 1912. From 1913 until 1919 'D. Bannerman, probationer' was the stated supply. Mr Bannerman, born in 1835, had been admitted as a probationer in 1894 but was not eligible for calls. He died in August 1919 aged 84.[43]

An account of the 1920 Synod meeting stated: 'Rev. E. MacQueen[44] brought before the Synod the question of the supply of Beauly and Daviot, and suggested that Mr William Macdonald, elder, Inverness, should be appointed as regular missionary for these places. Rev. Neil Cameron moved that the appointment be made. The motion was seconded by the

---

[42] This was probably John MacAulay (1853–1943), who served as missionary in a number of places in Skye, including Broadford, Luib, and Elgol, but mainly in Applecross, Wester Ross. 'John MacAulay, Applecross', *FPM* Vol. 48 (July 1943): pp. 54–57.

[43] Rev. James Sinclair noted in Mr Bannerman's obituary: 'He was a man of superior intellect and refinement, a truly exercised Christian. His preaching was in a marked degree experimental, and was often very helpful to God's people. Though, owing to a constitutional infirmity, he was never called to the regular ministry, he did useful service in his day, and his memory will be cherished with respect by not a few.' 'The late Rev. D. Bannerman, Conon Bridge', *FPM* Vol. 24 (October 1919): p. 191.

[44] Ewen MacQueen (1866–1949) was from Skye. He served as minister of Harris from 1901 to 1903, then the joint Lairg-Rogart-Dornoch-Bonar charge from 1903 until 1912. Mr MacQueen then pastored Kames from 1912 to 1919. He became minister of Inverness in 1919, where he remained until leaving the denomination in 1938. In that year he set up the 'Free Presbyterian Church 1893' for his supporters in Inverness. A. McPherson (editor), *History of the Free Presbyterian Church of Scotland: 1893–1970*, (Inverness: Publications Committee, Free Presbyterian Church of Scotland, 1975), pp. 175–177, 181–182.

Rev. M. Morrison,[45] and unanimously agreed to.'[46] Mr Mac-
Donald died in 1923.[47] It would seem that Mr MacDonald had
as his fellow labourer Angus Stewart (1859–1938), who was
listed as missionary for Beauly and Daviot from 1921 to
1923.[48] Hugh Munro then served Beauly and Daviot from
around 1924 until around 1936.[49] The Dingwall elder Kenneth
Matheson[50] would almost certainly have helped Mr Munro
supply Beauly.

Alex began conducting services sometime in the early to
mid 1930s. In a note of the event he recalled:

> I now feel my need of preparation for the Sabbath, in some
> respects as much as I did the first day I went to speak to my
> fellow creatures. I'll always remember that day and ever will,
> because I got such a fright. Rev. D.A. Macfarlane and Finlay

---

[45] Murdo Morrison (1877–1947) was from Barvas, Lewis. He was
minister of Glendale from 1909 to 1913, when he became pastor of
Lochinver. In 1934 he left Lochinver for the Raasay charge where
he served for a year and then retired due to ill-health to Tain. 'The
late Rev. Murdo Morrison, Tain, Ross-shire', *FPM* Vol. 52 (August
1947): pp. 70–72.

[46] 'Meeting of Synod', *FPM* Vol. 25 (July 1920): pp. 69–70.

[47] Mr MacDonald served as joint missionary in Beauly and Tomatin.
'William MacDonald, Missionary, Tomatin', *FPM* Vol. 28 (January
1924): pp. 285–286.

[48] Mr Stewart's presentation of Bible truth was described as 'ready
and apt'. 'The late Mr Angus Stewart, Elder, Inverness', *FPM* Vol.
44 (October 1939): pp. 223–227.

[49] Mr Munro was first listed as being missionary in 1925 in 'Tabular
View of Sustentation Fund and Special Collections of the Free Pres-
byterian Church of Scotland', *FPM* Vol. 30 (July 1925): pp. 94–95.
See also 'The late Mr Hugh Munro, Missionary', *FPM* Vol. 46
(November 1941): pp. 170–171.

[50] 'The late Mr Kenneth Matheson, Elder, Dingwall', *FPM* Vol. 48
(January 1944): pp. 170–171.

Beaton[51] called at our house. The minister said, 'You have to go to Fort William for the Sabbath.' I replied that I could not undertake anything like that. If anyone was in earnest, I was. Mr Macfarlane did not appear to have any mercy for me. He took out a slip of paper, wrote on it, and said, 'That is the address where you will stay.' I felt like someone pushed into the deep water of a harbour, and allowed to get out of it the best way he could.[52]

In 1936 the Synod agreed to appoint Alex to supply Beauly and Daviot on alternate Sabbaths 'as a temporary arrangement'.[53] Alex Maclennan began work as missionary at a time when the Beauly congregation had been weakened by the deaths of two godly men—Peter Stewart and William MacDonald (Kirkhill). Stewart had been influenced by the preaching of Dr Kennedy and by a close friendship with Simon Campbell (Brolan) in whose house weekly meetings were conducted.[54]

Alex's work as a missionary was to prove anything but temporary, although his responsibilities outside Beauly changed, with the focus shifting to help hold services in Dingwall. This, along with the efforts of other office-bearers in

---

[51] Finlay Beaton (1883–1974) was an elder in Inverness and one of the best known office-bearers in the north. He was a missionary for Stratherrick and a regular visitor at communion seasons across the Highlands and in the Isle of Lewis. 'Mr Finlay Beaton, Inverness', FPM Vol. 83 (September 1978): pp. 243–246.

[52] Diary, Saturday 20th October 1956.

[53] In 'Meeting of Synod', FPM Vol. 41 (January 1937): pp. 366–367.

[54] 'The late Mr Peter Stewart, Kilmorack', FPM Vol. 37 (February 1933): pp. 423–424. 'The late Mr Wm. Macdonald, Kilmorack', ibid.: pp. 424–425. Scoraig native Simon Campbell (1856–1932) was a shepherd and noted for his happy demeanour. 'The late Mr Simon Campbell, Beauly', FPM Vol. 39 (July 1934): pp. 154–155. Brolan is probably Broallan, a small scattering of houses near Balblair.

the area, proved to be a great help to the Rev. Donald A. Macfarlane.

The Rev. Donald A. Macfarlane with his first wife,
Catherine Cameron from Oban
Photo: Rev. J. Tallach

The people connected to the joint charge of Dingwall and Beauly lived across a large swathe of south-east Ross and north-eastern Inverness-shire. West coast pupils resident during term time in the hostel in Dingwall swelled the numbers. Dingwall had around a hundred people attending in the 1960s with sixty to seventy regularly at the Beauly services. A growth in the numbers attending the Beauly prayer meetings can be traced in these diaries but this reflects increased car ownership rather than implying a lower tempo of spiritual life there in the early years.

Before weekly Gaelic services were discontinued in 1959 in Beauly, public worship in the Gaelic language took place at 11am on Sabbath followed by English at 12 noon, and by English again at 6pm. People queued keenly outside for the noon diet of worship. Gaelic preaching continued in Beauly at communion seasons for some time after that.

Mr Macfarlane preached on alternate Sabbaths in Dingwall or Beauly. In the early 1960s, two English services were held in each place, as well as a Sabbath Gaelic service in Dingwall for a few years after Beauly discontinued services in that language.

Mr Macfarlane was noted for his spiritually-minded preaching and personal godliness. However, he suffered from depression and was unable to carry out his duties for extended periods of time.[55] When he became ill, the doctor restricted him to preaching only once on Sabbath. As a result, Alex and John Maclennan and others had three English services to cover instead of the usual two.

Mr Macfarlane was very insistent on the duty of elders to be regularly visiting in the Beauly and Dingwall congregations. Alex and his brother John took this to heart, often visiting people together. Family worship conducted by Alex could have its challenges: although he would not closely question people, he would sometimes ask people what they thought of a particular verse in the passage read. Alex felt a particular

---

[55] Alex sometimes visited him during these periods around the time of family worship.

drawing to the travelling people and often visited their encampments to read the Bible and pray with them.

Alex married Elizabeth Mackenzie in 1949. She was a native of Shieldaig in Wester Ross, and worked as a district nurse.[56] He once said while conducting a service that 'a man may give all he has, and all he can get, to give all to his wife, but if he does not give her his heart and his love, it means nothing worthwhile and he does not love her as he should. So it is with us and the Lord Jesus.' A diary note on a wedding anniversary was typical of such entries. 'I am seven years married today, seven is a perfect number. I have not hitherto regretted the step I took. It was, I think, the happiest period of my life.'[57]

Speaking from the Word of God

Alex had a good grasp of doctrine and experience and read much in Christian literature. A favourite author was the Puritan, Thomas Goodwin.[58] This all impacted on how he explained the Word of God in taking services. An obituary stated: 'Being possessed of a most retentive memory and a keen intellect allied to the sensitive ear of a poet and the acute eye of an artist, he was a master of apt illustrations as he elo-

---

[56] She was born on 14th September 1903 and died on 7th August 1999. After Alex's death, Bessie married an elder in the Lochcarron congregation, John Mackenzie of Kishorn. She was buried in Kishorn cemetery. Alex often addressed her in letters as Eliza while many people in the community and church knew her as Bessie.

[57] Diary, Thursday 12th April 1956.

[58] Thomas Goodwin (1600–1680) was a preacher and writer, the president of Magdalen College in Oxford, and a chaplain to Oliver Cromwell. He was a contemporary of John Owen. Goodwin was a member of the Westminster Assembly and a leading Independent. His *Works* have been frequently reprinted.

quently proclaimed the gospel message of salvation for even the chief of sinners in and by the risen Christ.'[59]

People who heard him conduct services can still recall his vivid word pictures. He once spoke of the forbidding appearance of the mountain Suilven in western Sutherland, when viewed from the sea as one sailed towards land. There were dark steep cliffs and difficult terrain to face if a person tried to climb it from the shore. But if you headed toward Suilven from inland, it was a more gently rising slope without the forbidding difficulty of the coastal approach. He compared this to the view the sinner has by nature of an unapproachable and stern God of justice, until enlightened by the Holy Spirit to see that in Christ there is a gentle and welcoming approach in the very same God.

He was once speaking of those who mock the idea of the resurrection of the dead. They mock the concept of bodies, which have turned to dust and spread through the earth, being brought together again at the Judgment Day. Alex's answer to that was that if iron filings were in the ground, no human could gather them, but a powerful magnet would soon grab every last one out of the soil. If a mere magnet could do that, how much more could the divine power gather the dust of people's bodies together and bring them to life.

During the 1960s, he once spoke to a friend about the decline of the gospel in various areas of the country. He spoke of how Thomas Boston[60] had seen much fruit in Ettrick: it

---

[59] *Ross-shire Journal*, Friday 14th January 1972, p. 9.

[60] Thomas Boston (1676–1732) was minister of Simprin and later of Ettrick. He is known today as the author of books such as *Human Nature In Its Four-fold State*, *A View of the Covenant of Grace*, *The Crook in the Lot* and many others. In 1718 he was involved in the controversial republication of *The Marrow of Modern Divinity*, a Puritan compilation dating to 1645.

lingered a while and then died out. He then spoke of Perthshire and the Loch Tay area where there had been great revivals in the early 1800s but where now, virtually nothing was left in terms of Reformed spirituality. He compared this phenomenon to a fire in a room. If a fire burned for a while in it, the room would be very warm, but if the fire went out, the apartment would very quickly become the coldest in the house.

During an Inverness communion season,[61] Alex spoke at the Question Meeting[62] and said that his Christian life began with the words 'God be merciful to me a sinner', and that he expected to end his Christian life having the same prayer, 'God be merciful to me a sinner.' He found useful lines of thought from texts discussed at the Question Meetings for his own subsequent exhortations about the Word of God. For example, at Dingwall on Sabbath 12th July 1959 he took the text which had been talked about at the Tain Question Meeting two days previously, Romans 7:24. 'O wretched man that I am! Who shall deliver me from the body of this death?' At the Beauly prayer meeting on Thursday 9th July that year, he

---

[61] The 'season' is made up of preparatory services running from Thursday to Saturday, followed by the sacrament dispensed on Sabbath morning, a service with a gospel message in the evening, and concluding with the thanksgiving service(s) on the Monday.

[62] This meeting, also known as the fellowship meeting, takes place on the Friday of the communion season, a day set apart for self-examination. It involves discussion of evidences of conversion using a suitable text from the Bible known as 'the Question'. An elder proposes the text, a minister then makes introductory remarks ('opening the Question'), several professing men 'speak to the Question' as requested by the presiding minister and another minister, if available, 'closes the Question' by making concluding remarks (and corrections if necessary).

took the portion of Scripture spoken to at Beauly's own Question Meeting the previous week.

One day he went to a friend's house in Easter Ross, from where he was to get a lift to the Bonar Bridge communion services. His friend, a young man, expressed great fear about the possibility of being asked to speak to the Question. A little later, Alex asked if he could be given a place to be on his own for a few minutes, so he was shown to a room. After Alex returned, the young man went to the room and found a sheet of paper in Alex's handwriting, giving four points relating to marks of grace. The man felt this was an attempt to help a young person in a nerve-racking situation and that it showed Alex's thoughtfulness.

A young man who had recently professed had been asked to pray frequently within a short space of time. This was because he was due to move soon afterwards to a place with almost no praying men, and might benefit from being used to doing so. The young man was concerned that pride might creep in because of this. He expressed this fear to Alex, who said, 'You know that no matter how good the food you give it, the pig will still put its foot into the trough.'

He once used the following illustration:

> There was a deep gorge with two boards across it. One was strong and safe; the other appeared to be so too, but wasn't. It had rotten parts, and as soon as you stepped on it you were down and lost.

His word pictures could be graphic and applied personally to the congregation. A regular hearer recalled him saying:

> Are you leaning on Christ with all your weight? Is it as if you are leaning over the side of a ship, and are held up by a spar of wood? A sailor in this situation knows that there is nothing

but that spar of wood which is standing between him and falling into the deep. Are you leaning on him with the knowledge that, if it were not for him, you would be lost?

There was a large water butt at the end of Alex's house which collected the rain which ran off the roof. There was no water supply on the croft in earlier days and the cattle would often come to the water butt in particularly dry weather. But there was one Highland cow in the herd. Her long horns meant that when the water level would go down, she couldn't get her head far enough into the barrel to drink. Alex said this was like people and the gospel—the horns of pride and unbelief meant they wouldn't partake of the water of life for the soul.

Alex also used homely analogies:

> In the old days, in the Highlands, it used to be said that you knew there was life still in a home when you saw a puff of smoke rising from a chimney. In a similar way, when there is the smoke of prayer rising up to heaven, that is a sign of spiritual life in that person's heart.

A member of one of the sects knocked on his door and told him their views. Alex listened and then told them that although there might be some sound links in a ship's chain, even one flawed link would put it on the rocks.

A description he gave of a person in doctrinal error was to compare them to someone trying to fix a light bulb on a high ceiling. First they'd try standing on a table, then put a box on top of it, and when they still couldn't reach, a chair might be put on the box. It would be a very dangerous foundation, he added.

He once had an illustration of the fact that we are not capable of overcoming sin in our hearts and lives in our own strength:

> There was a hunter once who got hold of the tail of a snake and he was pulling with all his strength to get the snake out of the hole where it was hiding. What this man did not realise was that, in the depths of that hole, the snake was curled several times round the root of a tree and its head was out the other side, laughing at the man who thought that he could pull it out.

Referring to people who came regularly to church but took no interest in their own souls, he often told them they were like a hinge on a door—it came, it went, but got no further forward. He had an instinct for how people felt about their advancing years but had a message of hope for them: 'People don't like getting old and grey. But if you are in Christ, friend, cheer up! You'll be youthful and buoyant for ever.'

Alex was always short when leading in prayer. His speaking about the Word of God in church was described by one hearer as 'beautiful, most engaging, he never wearied you'. He had a natural style and modulated his voice nicely.

Alex would lose no opportunity to spread the good news of the Word of God. Before Gift Aid,[63] giving to charities as a wage earner was a complicated process. One step was submitting a certificate signed by the church stating what had been donated. Alex would write on the back of his certificate: 'What shall it profit a man, though he gain the whole world, and lose his own soul?' At a Laide (Wester Ross) communion

---

[63] A scheme through which registered charities can reclaim tax on a donation made by a UK taxpayer, so adding to its value.

season, two little girls were playing, one of whom wore a red dress with a white band on it. Alex came up to them and said: 'Your sins are as scarlet as that dress, but Christ can make them as white as that braid.'

Alex was a 'character' with a slight strain of eccentricity. He would cycle to church wearing his suit, coat and hat, but with his hands in his pockets as he cycled along. He once left the elder's seat at a Question Meeting to hand a sweet to the man who had just finished speaking, so pleased was he with the man's contribution. As he became progressively deaf, it was not unknown for a person leading in prayer at church to finish and open their eyes—only to find Alex standing beside him in order to hear him. Every morning in Tomich, he would throw the window open and sing Psalm 117.

He also had a sense of humour. He once spoke of a steamer which had berthed at a West Highland pier. The Captain had grown impatient as the tourists failed to return at the set time. He blew the ship's whistle loudly for so long that there wasn't enough steam left in the boiler for the ship to move. Alex added that the incident was like Arminian preaching: there was a lot of noise but no real progress.

He used the steamship analogy in a more solemn warning too, when he said:

> The hypocrite is like the steamship which was sailing on the Great Lakes. It sounded its siren to tell the passengers that it was about to leave the pier. However, when the passengers had got aboard, it transpired that the ship had used so much steam announcing its departure that it had no steam left to pull away from the pier.

He could be at the receiving end of good-humoured teasing. On one occasion he was at a communion in Shieldaig. His wife had recently bought him a present of an electric razor. Alex anxiously asked Rev. D.R. MacDonald[64] what the voltage was in the Shieldaig electricity supply. The minister replied: 'I'll tell you what we'll do, Alex. We'll go and see what voltage we can get out of all the elders and missionaries who're at the manse.'

It was recalled that Alex 'could be disconcertingly out-spoken as occasion demanded'.[65] However, he was known to occasionally go slightly beyond the boundaries of his church's insistence on Scriptural standards of dress and appearance. He was known to have been reprimanded privately by at least two ministers for his frequently expressed dislike of the colour red in professing men's ties. He sometimes made comments about the colour of young women's clothing that might have been more appropriately made, if relevant, by an older woman. Young men who had just professed faith resisted his view that they should begin wearing a hat on the way to church; his jus-tification being that they could then show respect and rever-ence by removing the headgear at the church door.

Alex was naturally assertive in his bearing and speech, in contrast to the quieter style of many Highland elders of the era. This enabled him to strike up conversations with complete strangers about their souls. A shrewd ability for church exten-sion was shown when he guided a West Coast family looking for a croft in the eastern Highlands (for health reasons) to a holding within the catchment area of the Beauly congregation. He knew when not to impose himself on people of his own church who he sensed were nervous around senior figures.

---

[64] Donald Roderick Macdonald (1887–1963) served in Tarbert, Isle of Harris, from 1927 until 1951; after that he was pastor of Shieldaig from 1951 until 1963. 'Tribute to Rev. D.R. Macdonald, Shieldaig', *FPM* Vol. 68 (May 1963): pp. 28–29.

[65] *Ross-shire Journal*, Friday 14th January 1972, p. 9.

He was perhaps more self-confident in public than others, but had a low opinion of his own spiritual progress. He once wrote:

> Here I am at the end of the year. The question is: what have I gained? To be honest, all I can say is that I am daily sinking down in humiliation and self-loathing for the sins and errors of my youth. What a slothful servant I am in the Master's service, feeling hardness of heart, the Bible to be a sealed book, clad with the armour of Diabolus,[66] having a dumb and prayerless spirit, and oppressed with spiritual poverty. I am thirsting after the sense of assurance. I feel I must keep praying in such a condition. I can, however, say that Christ is rising in my estimation as the years pass.[67]

Death

During his final illness, on the last night that he was able to sleep upstairs, he told those helping him on the stair: 'I'll soon be going up to a better place.' He died on 1st January 1972.

In a letter of sympathy to Elizabeth, written after the funeral, Rev. Alexander McPherson (Stratherrick)[68] wrote:

> When I arrived at Tomich today there was such a large crowd of mourners that I made no attempt to push my way through; and in any case, I felt that my and my wife's sympathy might

---

[66] Diabolus is a leading character in John Bunyan's allegory, *The Holy War*, originally published in 1682. Diabolus overcomes the town of Man-soul but is eventually defeated by Emmanuel.

[67] Diary, Thursday 22nd November 1956.

[68] Alexander McPherson (1915–2000) served on the Church's Rhodesia mission from 1947 as a builder and lay missionary. Following divinity training he was ordained and inducted in 1961, holding pastorates successively at Dornoch-Rogart, Farr-Stratherrick-Tomatin, London, and Perth. 'The late Rev. Alexander McPherson, Perth', *FPM* Vol. 106 (March 2001): pp. 84–86.

be better expressed in a note than by a brief handshake, one among many at a time when you would scarcely take in what was happening. When I first sampled life in the north of Scotland during my period of study in 1960, I was much impressed with the individuality of the 'men' and their obvious grace and kindliness. Your late husband was one of those. By any standard he was an outstanding Christian; and now that the Lord who made him so, has taken him to the better country, we have no reason to sorrow as far as he is concerned. Christ's cause is poorer and you are poorer, but the Lord who gave and took away can sustain and comfort you, and we trust he will. Perhaps you will also mention to John that we sympathise with him also.

Rev. Malcom MacSween, Oban,[69] wrote to Elizabeth:

We were deeply grieved to hear of the death of your beloved husband who was also a dear friend of ours. Though we heard of his illness yet we were hearing of a partial recovery and we were certainly hoping to have him left with us but that was not the will of the Lord. No. But the Lord took him to be forever with himself. For this he had been preparing for many a day and now that he is in the glory of heaven we mourn his loss, even though we know he is inconceivably happier than he could ever have been in this world.

Your dear husband was a burning and a shining light in the Lord's vineyard. The darker the day, the more brightly the Lord's dear people shine in his service. When I heard of his departure I thought of his receiving these words from the Master, 'Well done, good and faithful servant.' It is sore to lose our dear ones, but O, may we be prepared as they were!

---

[69] Mr MacSween (1904–1978) was a highly respected pastor and Old Testament tutor in the Free Presbyterian Church. 'The Late Rev. Malcolm MacSween, M.A.', *FPM* Vol. 85 (March 1980): pp. 85–89.

Dear Mrs Maclennan, may the Lord hold you up in this time of your great loss and sorrow! We are very much with you in our thoughts.

The supreme court of his church, the annual Synod, published a tribute to him:

> As a member of this Court on numerous occasions he discharged his duties with faithfulness and willingness. In public and in private Mr Maclennan gave clear evidence that his treasure was in Heaven and that his affections were set on things above. Being observant of the signs of the times he was frequently grieved by the declension of religion in the land. On the other hand he looked for and longed for the promised revival of the cause of Christ. [...] In this day of small things his passing away is a grievous loss to the Church below.[70]

NORMAN CAMPBELL
STORNOWAY

---

[70] 'Tribute to the late Mr Alexander Maclennan, Elder, Dingwall and Beauly', *Synod Proceedings, May, 1972* (Glasgow, 1972), pp. 32–33.

Autobiography: 'He led me'

'I felt the drawing power of his love'

I NEED the grace of God and unfeigned humility to undertake writing a little about myself. I heard it said, 'There is no love on earth so sincere as the love creatures bear to themselves.' Also the Scriptures say, 'The heart is deceitful above all things, and desperately wicked.' So, I need wisdom and much grace, and to be ruthless towards myself in stating the truth about my conversion.

Early spiritual experiences

I spent about twenty-three years of my life like a wild ass's colt on the mountains of vanity. I ransacked sea and land looking for satisfaction, till at last I found myself as silly as the donkeys in Italy, about which Thomas Goodwin speaks. When the driver wished the beast to move faster he tied a pole to the cart with a bundle of hay sticking to the end of it and reaching about two feet in front of the donkey's nose. The donkey could not get any nearer, no matter how fast it walked. I came at last to the conclusion that no lasting happiness could be found on earth. 'He who builds under the sky builds too low.'[71]

I took to reading the Bible, especially the New Testament. I thought that I really believed that the same Jesus I was reading about made the spacious sea I was sailing on. That made it interesting to me.

I was lodging once with an atheist who did his best to convert me to his view. At last he said: 'I can make nothing of you. They gave you bad milk to begin with.' This shows how useful it is for our young people to be well grounded in the Psalms of David and the Catechisms.[72]

I then took a liking for works of divines, especially Dr Thomas Goodwin, they being the first that came to my hands. I loved to read his books on holiness in heart and life.[73] I really do hope to meet him in heaven. I was at his grave in the Bunhill Cemetery[74] in the middle of London. I noticed that the bombs which fell thick did not touch his grave. The name of Dr Thomas Goodwin is fragrant to me whenever I hear it mentioned.

---

[71] Possibly an adaptation of a verse in *Night Thoughts* by Edward Young (1683–1765), Fellow of All Souls, Oxford, known as a poet, critic and philosopher: 'Too low they build, who build beneath the stars'.

[72] The Larger and Shorter Catechisms of the Westminster Assembly of Divines.

[73] This is probably a reference to Goodwin's *Gospel Holiness in Heart and Life* in Volume 7 of his *Works*, which focuses on Philippians 1:9–11.

[74] Bunhill Fields is a former non-denominational burial ground in the London Borough of Islington. It was in use from 1665 until 1854. Many Nonconformists were buried there, including John Bunyan, John Gill, John Owen and Isaac Watts. The burial ground was badly damaged by bombing during World War II.

I may describe my conversion in these particulars. It was a gradual, protracted work by the Word and the Spirit of God.

1. I believed the record God gave concerning his Son Jesus Christ.

2. I came to see the spirituality of the law of God—its length and breadth, and extensive compass, reaching into the innermost recesses of my being, thoughts, words, motives, spirit—to my very nature.

3. I began to pray, which was a most pleasant exercise in those early days of my Christian pilgrimage. It is recorded of Paul after Christ met him on the Damascus road, 'Behold, he prayeth.' I can still remember the prayer my mother taught me when going to bed at four years of age: 'Dèan tròcair orm-sa a tha am pheacach, agus glan mi ann am fuil Chrìosda.'[75] I cannot get a better one to this day. I feel my profound need of it. Someone said: 'It is not easy to make a man begin to pray, but when he once begins, it is not easy to make him stop.' My opinion is, that whoever has the life of God within, he will persevere at it to the end.

4. I began to associate with the people of God. They were the only company I delighted in, although at times I was afraid of them lest they should ask me to engage in a duty for which I had no strength. Someone said that 'all on the way to heaven must pass Sinai and Calvary, though all do not get the same distinct view of them'. I cannot speak of the terrors of Sinai, nor do I consider that experience necessary to salvation. I can only say that I felt an extraordinary measure of the drawing power of God's everlasting love and great meltings of soul in secret prayer.

---

[75] 'Have mercy on me, a sinner, and cleanse me in the blood of Christ.'

All I can say about my prayers in those days is that they were sweeter to me than my literal food. My eyes were a fountain of tears, but, alas, these warm pleasant feelings subsided after a few years. If you should ask what is my position now that these feelings are gone, my answer is: 'We walk by faith not by sight.' I can say:

(a) My estimation of Christ is increasing. The overtowering wonder to me is 'God manifest in the flesh'.

(b) I sink down more and more in humiliation and self-loathing.

(c) God's sovereignty frightens me when I consider how God pitched on me, and left multitudes to perish.

(d) I earnestly desire to have a place in the everlasting love of God (Psalm 91), to be under the shelter of Christ's wings. 'This is all my salvation and all my desire.'

Hardships in Providence

I had a trying time during the Depression of the peace years between the two wars. The reason I bring that in is to magnify the Lord. I was often without any source of water within the radius of a mile, for man or beast, and had to cart it in casks. I could only make my request known to God whom I believed was the Creator of every fountain of water. In his good time he answered me. I now desire to praise his name every time I open a tap, enjoying abundance of excellent water.

Scarcity of money

I could not pay my way for want of money—I would dread going over it again. I earnestly asked the Lord to give me a handful of 'the dust of the earth' to pay my liabilities. He has done it. Praise his holy name. 'The silver and the gold is mine.' I believed all the time that to him belonged the silver and the gold, and the cattle on a thousand hills. Many an errand it gave me to the throne of grace, that I was so pressed in the Lord's providence.

My prayers are now turned into praise for what he has done for me. I regard his goodness as a token of his everlasting love. I feel that it should lead me to repentance, and to honour God with my substance. I believe that God has no pleasure in afflicting men if they would learn wisdom at a cheaper rate.

Alas, the sunshine of prosperity has the tendency to make men forgetful of God and their latter end, so that those whom he expects to save generally get knocks to wean them from this earth and from 'the love of the world'. Now, many would say as to the change in my outward circumstances that we have sailed into 'better times' in a 'stroke of good luck'. If only they would realise how much they dishonour God. May we learn the art of 'seeing God in everything'. I myself share the feeling of the poet who said, 'Every prospect pleases, only man is vile.'[76]

I desire that my mouth may be filled with the high praises of the Lord for the many answers he gave to my prayers, and I also now praise him for the cases in which he did not grant my request. Subsequent events proved God's goodness in keeping certain things from me. 'No man knows what is good for him in this life.'[77]

---

[76] The words are in the second verse of *From Greenland's icy mountains*, a hymn by Richard Heber, Anglican Bishop of Calcutta (1783–1826). 'What though the spicy breezes / blow soft o'er Ceylon's isle; / though every prospect pleases, / and only man is vile: in vain with lavish kindness / the gifts of God are strown; / the heathen in his blindness / bows down to wood and stone.'

[77] 'For who knoweth what is good for man in this life, all the days of his vain life which he spendeth as a shadow? for who can tell a man what shall be after him under the sun?' (Ecclesiastes 6:12).

Looking for another place

Having seafaring experience, I applied for a job on the Caledonian Canal. The Engineer at Clachnaharry[78] was quite pleased with my papers, but told me that usually the son took over from the father, so that it was difficult for a stranger to get in. I applied afterwards for a janitor's job, but it ended in disappointment.

I did my utmost on several occasions to get away from No. 1 Tomich[79] and, to be sure, I prayed much about the matter, but the Lord in infinite wisdom did not hearken to me. Even Moses, the man of God, was once told: 'Speak no more to me of this matter.' God had another plan for my life, as subsequent events showed. Our safety lies in committing our way to God. I have learned that lesson by hard experience. Truly we need patience and much grace when, as Dr Kennedy said, 'There is snow in the profession, frost in the affections, and hailstones in God's providence.' 'Who in its cold can live?'[80] Jacob said, 'All these things are against me.'

I thought often that I could not be in a worse place than I fell into [...] 45 acres of impossible soil, without any reliable source of water, and not a tree in the whole area for shade or shelter! However, I came to see that there was no better in the whole estate for me than this one. So I always believe that the Lord will carve out for one, better than he would himself, when one trusts him and asks for his guidance and blessing. I discovered myself that my holding was the best.

About the year 1950 I was approached by the Logan firm who asked if I were willing to give them ten acres of my hold-

---

[78] The Clachnaharry Works are situated at the north end of the canal, where it joins the Beauly Firth.
[79] Alex's home near Muir of Ord.
[80] Psalm 147:17, metrical version.

ing for a yard and garage. I at first declined to grant it, but told them that, if they were unsuccessful elsewhere, I would be prepared to discuss the matter with them again. They came again, and I agreed to let them have ten acres of my holding, on condition that they would do no unnecessary work on the Sabbath days, provide for me a supply of water in that field, and suitable compensation, to which the firm agreed. Shortly after that, William Logan sent a huge mechanical digger, and within two hours struck water at 18 feet. In due time, he put a tap into my field, and latterly to my house. So things have gone well with me since Logan's entry.

I have often thought how wise and well provided for they are, who allow Christ into their hearts. 'If any man open the door, I will come in and sup with him, and he with me.' I got abundance of excellent water by letting Logan in. To those who let Christ into their hearts, the truth will be fulfilled: 'The water that I give him shall be in him a well of water springing up unto eternal life.'

Following the means

The old fathers used to say, when asked their opinion of such a person, 'He is following the means whatever.'[81] 'He that walketh with wise men shall be wise' [Proverbs 13:20]. I began to see the means of grace in a new light. When I think of my former ways, I see the attitude I bore to the means was vanity, carnality, profound ignorance of the gospel, indifference, all bodily exercise and lip service. I just wonder, when I look back, that I was not struck dead. How I magnify God's

---

[81] He used a literal English translation of the Gaelic word 'co-dhiù': idiomatic English would be 'He is following the means [of grace] at any rate.'

grace now in calling me out of such a state in which I would have perished eternally! 'He is rich in mercy.'

Along with following the means, I felt the main current of my affections turning towards heavenly things, and I began to look to the things that are eternal. I lost appetite for vain company and vain conversation. My desire was as much as possible to be with the people of God.

Witnessed publicly

I was following the means of grace for about fifteen years prior to coming forward to church membership. Some of the Lord's people were asking me what was keeping me back. One godly woman said to me at the fireside, 'Why don't you witness for Christ?' I could hardly get an answer. The words stuck to me.

The day after, I was listening to Hugh Munro, missionary, Beauly, at the prayer meeting. He was speaking from the book of Jonah and in the course of his lecture, referring to Jonah's disobedience, he came out with these words, 'And if the Lord will rise up against you for not doing your duty, how are you to get out of his hand?' I felt it was directed to me, and I could not shake it off.

When I came before the Kirk Session for membership, I had no truth to give that induced me to come, only that I saw divine authority stamped on every page of the Bible, that I was led to see my exceeding sinfulness, and that I had no righteousness in myself (more than Satan) in which to stand before a holy God. I came to see the spirituality of the Law in such a measure that my only hope for eternity was based on the unspotted righteousness of Jesus Christ.

I was impressed once with a verse I saw on a calendar. I never forgot it:

Under an eastern sky,
Amidst a rabble cry,
A man went forth to die
FOR ME.[82]

The Lord may bless what is agreeable to his Word.

Began to preach[83]

I will never forget one morning a minister and an elder came along to my house in the month of March 1936. They said to me: 'You have to supply [take the services] in Fort William next Sabbath.' I protested vigorously, and told them I was not at all for that work. I felt like a man pushed over the pier head and told: 'Sink or swim.' Instead of listening to my protests, the minister took a paper from his pocket and wrote the address where I was to stay in Fort William. So I had to bow to this dispensation of God's providence.

It appears that God had a plan for my life, because after I started with the Lord's work, the tide turned in my favour in providence. Should we not regard it as an honour to be employed in his service, and seek grace to keep our garments clean, to adorn the gospel of our Lord and Saviour?

When I started first, I had great difficulty in overcoming self-consciousness, but it seems clear to me that the Master had work for me to do when I got over it, as I was afraid that I would never do so—namely to stand before two hundred people and speak without fear. A godly man told me that, though he had enough matter beforehand, if he was suddenly called in public to speak, it would all leave him. The strong (I

---

[82] The opening verse of a hymn by John Long, published in 1917.

[83] As indicated in the preface, 'preaching' is not a term normally used for the address during public worship given by an elder or missionary in the Free Presbyterian Church.

suppose) cannot understand such. It seems the Lord sees good to empty some of his people of creature strength.

However, though I got over that difficulty, what came in its place was no easier. Namely, deadness, the Bible a sealed book, God silent, having the greatest difficulty in settling on a passage, feeling like 'a reed shaken in the wind', feeling like one that did not know where to begin or to end, saying to myself, 'Is the cause to be entrusted to such a one as I am?'

I would be ashamed that my fellow creatures would know how unprepared I feel for Sabbath duties. Although the Lord carries me through in a manner surprising to myself on the Sabbath, when the next weekend approaches the clouds begin to gather again. From Wednesday onwards I feel a heavy burden on me, which I cannot shake off, so that the Sabbath which ought to be delightsome is not the joy I would like and ought to have like the Psalmist (Psalm 122).

However, it becomes me to say more to God's praise. He has held up my goings. I have not yet been struck dumb in front of my fellows, as I deserved. I learned more and more that there is nothing in mere words, and that what may please myself may not please my hearers. So I unreservedly cast myself upon the Lord, as we are commanded: 'Cast thou thy burden on the Lord.' I tell you, many a time when I look at the wall clock after the second singing,[84] and know that I am expected to speak so long, I just wonder where it is to come from. How can one of ordinary ability and such limited

---

[84] Public worship in the Free Presbyterian Church begins with congregational singing of verses from a Scottish Metrical Psalm, with a precentor leading the *a capella* praise. This is followed by an extempore prayer and a reading from the Authorised Version of the Bible. After the congregation sings a second Psalm, the minister or elder gives an address, after which there is an extempore prayer and the service ends by singing further verses of a Psalm.

vocabulary as I possess, continue for nearly an hour speaking? I feel often like the disciples when they said to Christ, 'Whence should we have bread to feed such a multitude?'

Some of the old fathers declared that however much they studied in the early part of their ministry, they came at last to a point when most of their preparation for the Sabbath was done on their knees. I heard of an eminent minister in Stoer, Sutherlandshire, of whom it was said that it would not be easy to get a private interview with him any time after Wednesday, so heavy the burden of the Sabbath lay on him. It is to be feared that it is a rare experience in our day. I would welcome if anyone relieved me when I am going to speak, if I thought that he had a spark of the grace of God. Paul himself had the fear that 'after having preached to others', he 'might be a castaway'. It seems the Lord keeps his people low, to give them errands to the throne of grace. I go there often because there is nothing else I can do about it.

I used to think that if I had more education and more extensive vocabulary, it would relieve me of my burden. Other times the thought would cross my mind: 'Why not rid yourself of that weekly burden by retiring?' I now suspect that these suggestions may have been from Satan. The danger which we wish to avoid by neglecting our duty, may meet us in the face. There is a safe spot, we are told, in the midst of the cyclone, 'where a leaf would not stir'. Someone has said in that connection: 'There is a safe spot also in every crisis that meets one in life. What is it? It is the path of duty.'

My paper is now done, so I bid you farewell meantime.

Diary

1957

Tuesday 1st January

I took the service today at Kilmorack from Psalm 98:1. 'O sing unto the Lord a new song; for he hath done marvellous things.' I remarked there was much singing of songs on such a day as this, New Year's Day. No one can sing this new song but new creatures, under a new covenant. Many of God's people had their day of singing vain songs; now they have a better song to sing, even the praises of his redeeming, electing and everlasting love, for the hope they have that he had called them by his grace, inclined them to love his ways and walk in the paths of new obedience. What wonders—the wonder of the incarnation besides which nothing else is worth mentioning.[85]

Wednesday 2nd January

In the book of Esther, we learn from the case of Haman the evil of pride, so that when he did not get the honour he expected, he was miserable. The danger of being lifted up in the ways of sin: 'Pride goeth before destruction.' We see also how God rules in providence. The Bible says Ahaseurus 'could not sleep'—a simple common occurrence, yet it was the first

---

[85] At the end of the service on 1st January he would always wish the people: 'A Happy New Year in the Lord!'

step in the salvation of the Jews. There is also a chain of events in the life of the believer. We learn also that it is never in vain to look to God. Scarcely was the outlook ever darker but they were saved. The shadow of death was turned to the morning.

Thursday 3rd January

Beauly prayer meeting, attendance nine. I took: 'I am Alpha and Omega, the beginning and the end' (Revelation 21:6). I spoke of the believer's desire to begin and end with Christ, praying for his guidance, blessing and protection before he embarks on any enterprise—then praising God for care, safety and success. He begins with Christ first thing in the morning and ends with Christ the last thing at night. He performs all duties in the strength and grace of Christ. He ascribes all he does to God's mercy. He is taught at the outset of his course to look to Christ. The end of the journey finds him still looking to him.

Sabbath 6th January.

Kilmorack. In the Gaelic I spoke of the new creature from 2 Corinthians 5. Points were:

1. What it is not.
2. Man has no hand in it.
3. It is the work of God.
4. The evidences of it.

The New Year will not be a blessing to us if we are not new creatures in Christ Jesus.

In the English I took Hebrews 8:10.[86] I remarked how desirable it was to begin a new year under the new covenant; otherwise we cannot have a blessing.

---

[86] 'For this is the covenant that I will make with the house of Israel after those days, saith the Lord; I will put my laws into their mind,

At 6pm my text was Hebrews 13:8. 'Jesus Christ, the same yesterday, and today and for ever.' In a world where all is fleeting and fluctuating, the soul of man needs some fixed principle to support it.

Thursday 17th January

I kept the prayer meeting in Dingwall from Romans 5:1.[87] I remarked that faith always has two companions: hope and love. Marks of those who are justified: they will condemn themselves; they will be daily seeking sanctification, aiming at holiness, purity and perfection; they will desire to grow in grace and conformity to the image of Christ.

Sabbath 20th January

Kilmorack. I took in Gaelic Matthew 21:44. 'On whomsoever it shall fall, it will grind him to powder.' I ventured to give it as my opinion that these are people who are 'exalted to heaven' with privileges such as communion seasons, familiar with 'the high things of Sion', the symbols of his body and blood but pass out of time in a state of impenitency.

In English I took Hebrews 3:1[88] and at 6pm took Psalm 91:2.[89] A rock is firm, unmovable by all the winds and waves that beat on it for a thousand years. The Word of God has withstood all the assaults of earth and hell.

---

and write them in their hearts: and I will be to them a God, and they shall be to me a people.'

[87] 'Therefore being justified by faith, we have peace with God through our Lord Jesus Christ.'

[88] 'Wherefore, holy brethren, partakers of the heavenly calling, consider the Apostle and High Priest of our profession, Christ Jesus.'

[89] 'I will say of the Lord, He is my refuge and my fortress: my God; in him will I trust.'

Friday 25th January

Inverness communion. The Question was given by Robert Watt[90] in Psalm 146:5. 'Happy is he that hath the God of Jacob for his help, whose hope is in the Lord his God.' I can't remember seeing so many strangers[91] at the Question Meeting for ten years. The assisting ministers are Mr MacLean, Ness,[92] and Mr MacQueen, London.[93]

Thursday 31st January

Dingwall communion. There was a gale this morning; the Inverness people could not come to Dingwall with trees across the road. Mr MacLean (Portree)[94] preached from Hebrews 2:1.[95]

---

[90] Robert Watt (1885–1966) was from Caithness and became an elder in Inverness. 'The late Mr Robert Watt, Elder, Inverness', *FPM* Vol. 72 (December 1967): pp. 233–237.

[91] An affectionate term for visitors from other congregations.

[92] William MacLean (1907–1985) became the Free Presbyterian missionary in Ness, Isle of Lewis, in 1941 and after divinity training served as its minister from 1948 to 1962. He then pastored Gisborne (New Zealand) from 1962 to 1973, Grafton (Australia) from 1973 to 1976, and returned to Ness for a second pastorate from 1976 to 1985. 'The late Rev. William MacLean M.A., Ness', *FPM* Vol. 90 (December 1985): pp. 378–385.

[93] John Peter MacQueen (1894–1961) was a Skye man who pastored the London congregation from 1936 until 1961. He remained in the city during the Blitz. He was a regular contributor to the denomination's magazine. 'The late Reverend John Peter MacQueen, London', *FPM* Vol. 67 (June 1962): pp. 37–42.

[94] Donald MacLean (1915–2010) was an accountant and served as a First Lieutenant in the Royal Navy in the Second World War. He was minister in Portree from 1948 to 1960 when he became pastor of the St Jude's (Glasgow) congregation until he retired in 2000. He served as Clerk of the Church's Synod from 1977 until 1989, as editor of *The Young People's Magazine* from 1949 to 1957, and as tutor in Systematic Theology from 1957 to 1986. 'Obituary: Rev.

Thursday 7th February

I kept the meeting in Kilmorack, the attendance was twelve. My text was Philippians 4:4–7.[96] Whichever way rejoicing is described, I think it cannot exist without peace, contentment and thankfulness. It is easier for the believer to say he has these than to say directly that he is rejoicing.

Sabbath 10th February

Dingwall. In the Gaelic I took Revelation 1, particularly the account of the appearance of Christ as John saw him in Patmos. What a change must come upon us before we can endure to see him as he is!

In English I took the church of Laodicea in Revelation 3. At 6.30 I continued in the same chapter (v. 18) on 'I counsel thee to buy of me gold tried in the fire'. I touched on a few points of similarity between literal gold and the grace of God, as well as points of contrast.

Donald MacLean', FPM Vol. 116 (October 2011): pp. 302–311. Reformation Press has published collections of his sermons: Unsearchable Riches (2013), Seeking a Better Country (2016) and Searched and Known (2018). It is intended to print further works.

[95] 'Therefore we ought to give the more earnest heed to the things which we have heard, lest at any time we should let them slip.'

[96] 'Rejoice in the Lord alway: and again I say, Rejoice. Let your moderation be known unto all men. The Lord is at hand. Be careful for nothing; but in every thing by prayer and supplication with thanksgiving let your requests be made known unto God. And the peace of God, which passeth all understanding, shall keep your hearts and minds through Christ Jesus.'

Tuesday 12th February

Today D. Mackenzie drove Mr Macfarlane, my wife and me up to Cannich.[97] We had a pleasant afternoon.

Thursday 14th February

This afternoon my wife and I visited old M who has taken a stroke. I am afraid his end is not far off but cannot tell how he stands for eternity, whether his foundation is sand or rock. He had an outward regard for the truth and ordinances all the years I knew him. What a solemn warning not to delay our repentance.

I took the Kilmorack prayer meeting (attendance sixteen) from Isaiah 60. I made some remarks about the glorious promises made to the church in the latter days. I said that if we do not see the Millennium we can have one now (praise his holy name!) if Christ is dwelling in our hearts.

Sabbath 17th February

I took the three services in Kilmorack today. Gaelic: Matthew 18:3.[98] English: John 6:37.[99] 6pm: Psalm 101, the leading points in the whole psalm.

---

[97] This was almost certainly to visit Angus MacInnes and his wife Mary Effie (née Campbell). Both were from Skye. They later moved to Torridon, Wester Ross. Mrs MacInnes was a sister of the Rev. Donald Campbell, Edinburgh. Their son Malcolm (Calum) MacInnes became minister in Ullapool and Toronto. Their daughter Mary became a teacher and married Rev. A.E.W. MacDonald, Gairloch. Mrs MacDonald died in 2015.

[98] 'And said, Verily I say unto you, Except ye be converted, and become as little children, ye shall not enter into the kingdom of heaven.'

[99] 'All that the Father giveth me shall come to me; and him that cometh to me I will in no wise cast out.'

Tuesday 19th February

Mr Macfarlane, my wife and I visited Seann Lios[100] and also James Forbes[101] in the afternoon. The minister read and sang in Psalm 72. Time is short, we must not miss any opportunity of doing good.

Thursday 21st February

Kilmorack prayer meeting (attendance eleven). It was a fine night as I cycled up in the gloaming. I was thinking to myself that I was in the best place on earth: I had plenty of time; it is within easy reach of a prayer meeting; God gave me a mind to attend it; the promise I have that God will be in the midst of us. Who ever heard the like? I know that is true and that I will never have to change my mind about it.

Sabbath 24th February

Dingwall. In Gaelic I took Luke 7:1–10.[102]

In English I took Isaiah 66:2.[103]

At 6.30 I took Psalm 118:24.[104] What is the day that the Lord hath made? It is the glorious Gospel Day, stretching from Eden in the first promise until all his elect are gathered from earth.

---

[100] A farm in Kiltarlity, home to the Fraser family.

[101] Mr Forbes, a retired crofter, died on 4th March 1965, aged 80. He lived at South Clunes near Kirkhill, Inverness-shire.

[102] The miracle of Christ healing the centurion's servant.

[103] 'For all those things hath mine hand made, and all those things have been, saith the Lord: but to this man will I look, even to him that is poor and of a contrite spirit, and trembleth at my word.'

[104] 'This is the day which the Lord hath made; we will rejoice and be glad in it.'

Sabbath 17th March

Kilmorack in the morning. In Gaelic I took John 10:25.[105]

In English I spoke of the slaughter weapons and the one with the inkhorn from Ezekiel 9:2.[106]

We had dinner at the Mission House and at 5pm went to read to them at Altyre, on the occasion of John's death.

At Dingwall in the evening as Mr Macfarlane has a pulpit announcement to make at Kilmorack. I took the curing of the leper in Matthew 8:1–4.

Wednesday 20th March

Today I attended the funeral of John Mackenzie, Altyre, from Struy, Strathglass. Rev. Mackay[107] began with prayer, I sang, putting out the line,[108] and Mr Macfarlane concluded. A

---

[105] 'Jesus answered them, I told you, and ye believed not: the works that I do in my Father's name, they bear witness of me.'

[106] 'And, behold, six men came from the way of the higher gate, which lieth toward the north, and every man a slaughter weapon in his hand; and one man among them was clothed with linen, with a writer's inkhorn by his side: and they went in, and stood beside the brasen altar.'

[107] Angus F. Mackay (1908–1996) became minister of Applecross in 1935 where he served until being called to Inverness in 1947. He remained pastor in the Highland capital until he retired in 1987. Mr Mackay was involved in tutoring divinity students from 1946 until 1981. 'The Rev. Angus Finlay Mackay, M.A. A Tribute', *FPM* Vol. 101 (October 1996): pp. 304–307.

[108] A method of singing where the line is first chanted ('given out') by the person leading the praise before the congregation sings it. The practice is to be found in English, German and Gaelic-speaking cultures. Sometimes two lines were given out. In some southern English churches of the Gospel Standard Strict Baptist tradition, the whole stanza was given out. Two such chapels in Sussex did so until the early 1980s; the last Gospel Standard church to do so was Salem Chapel, Carshalton, Surrey. The practice is examined in a book by Norman Campbell, *Reading the Line: An English-language lined-*

man came to me after the service, saying how he enjoyed
hearing the line given out as it reminded him of his childhood
days when they sang the Gaelic psalms. I believe personally the
line should be given out in a mixed crowd like that, gathered
on such an occasion. They cannot fail to receive some impression; at least they hear what is being sung.

Thursday 21st March

Kilmorack prayer meeting, attendance was thirteen. I took
the parable of the sower from Matthew 13. I compared literal
sowing to sowing to the Spirit. Both are done in faith, diligence, hope, patience and sacrifice.

Sabbath 24th March

Dingwall. In Gaelic my subject was the woman from the
coasts of Canaan in Matthew 15.

In English I had Ezekiel 11:19.[109]

At 6.30 I returned to the parable of the sower. Between
5pm and 6pm I went out to a field on the other side of the
railway to remonstrate with a group of young fellows playing
football. Shortly afterwards they left the field. May the Lord
bless the rebuke to them.

Sabbath 14th April

Kilmorack. I took in Gaelic John 12, 'I am come a light
into the world.' We had seven of a congregation.

In English I took the valley of dry bones from Ezekiel 37.
There is no case so desperate this side of the grave but there is

---

out Psalmody tradition in Presbyterian Scotland; (Stornoway: n.p.,
2005).
[109] 'And I will give them one heart, and I will put a new spirit within
you; and I will take the stony heart out of their flesh, and will give
them an heart of flesh.'

hope in God who can turn 'the shadow of death into the morning' [Amos 5:8].

At 6pm I took Matthew 28. I made some observations on the resurrection being the most important event of all time, and the foundation of the church. The Sabbath is the memorial of the resurrection, the keeping of which holy is a mark of a Christian.

Thursday 18th April

Prayer meeting, attendance was twelve. I took Mark 3:35.[110] In all the visible creation, man is the only rebel. What a humiliating thought for man created in the image of God! Man cannot be said to do the will of God until created anew.

Sabbath 21st April

Dingwall. I took in Gaelic the miracle of the loaves and fishes from Mark 6. Some points:

1. Much of the time had passed.
2. The desert place.
3. Christ's compassion and power displayed.

In English I took the last verse of Mark 3.

At 6.30pm I took the vision of the holy waters in Ezekiel 47. I made the waters to be the gospel. Water is indispensable to human life and comfort. We cannot do without the grace of God. Waters fertilise whatever else we have, they cleanse and beautify; so does the gospel of the grace of God wherever it comes. Some places were marshes or given to salt. Alas, many go to eternity from a gospel land without getting any good from it.

---

[110] 'For whosoever shall do the will of God, the same is my brother, and my sister, and mother.'

Sabbath 28th April

Kilmorack. In Gaelic I took 'I am the way, the truth and the life' in John 14:6. In the English I took Ezekiel 47 and the vision of the waters.

At 6pm I took blind Bartimaeus in Mark 10. I spoke of him as an emblem of the soul:

1. Blind in a spiritual sense, cannot see the danger nor the remedy.

2. Sight restored, crying for mercy, beginning to pray, seeing his condition and the glory of Christ.

3. He follows Christ.

Tuesday 30th April

Mrs Grant, Isabel, and Katie Chisholm called this evening with the recorder.[111] I gave a short discourse from John 4 on the analogy between literal water and the grace of God in Christ.

Thursday 2nd May

I had the prayer meeting in Dingwall as the minister was in Beauly. I made some observations from Mark 13 on the nature and duty of watchfulness.

---

[111] Mrs Isabella 'Bella' Grant (née Campbell) and her daughter Isabel of 4 Millburn Road, Inverness, recorded short devotional talks given by friends on a reel-to-reel tape recorder. These were sent to Mrs Grant's sister, Mrs Mary MacPherson, in New Zealand, for the benefit of the church people. Isabella and Mary were among the eleven children of James Campbell (1850–1932) an elder in Inverness and his wife Isabella. Another sister was Mrs Helen MacQueen, whose daughter Grace married Rev. Donald MacLean, Portree and Glasgow. Another sister, Rebecca, lived in Canada. For Mr Campbell, see 'The late James Campbell, Builder, Inverness', *FPM* Vol. 37 (August 1932): pp. 176–179. Isabel Grant was born in Inverness in 1927 and died on 6th September 2018.

Friday 3rd May

Isabel Grant came this evening and I gave a short discourse to the recorder from Acts 20:27.[112]

Sabbath 5th May

I took the Dingwall services. Gaelic: Mark 15:25. 'And it was the third hour and they crucified him.'

English: Hosea 2:19.[113] At 6.30 I took Luke 1:6. I made some remarks on:

1. Pharisaic righteousness.
2. The ceremonial law being inadequate.
3. The moral law condemning.
4. Gospel righteousness and justification.

Monday 6th May

Robert Ross, Rogart,[114] is being buried today. I feel so hard that I do not mourn as I should and as I would wish, that 'the righteous perisheth'. He was a pillar to the FP cause in that place. He was steadfast in the truth, on the side of all that was according to the Word of God.

Thursday 9th May

Kilmorack prayer meeting; attendance was 11. I took Hosea 8:14. 'For Israel hath forgotten his Maker, and buildeth temples.' Three points: forgetfulness of God, idolatry, and carnal confidence.

---

[112] 'For I have not shunned to declare unto you all the counsel of God.'

[113] 'And I will betroth thee unto me for ever; yea, I will betroth thee unto me in righteousness, and in judgment, and in lovingkindness, and in mercies.'

[114] 'Tribute to the Late Mr Robert Ross, Rogart', *Synod Proceedings, May, 1957* (Glasgow, 1957), p. 38.

Sabbath 12th May

Kilmorack. In Gaelic I took 2 Corinthians 5:17. 'If any man be in Christ, he is a new creature.' Points:

1. To be out of Christ is to be in a state of wrath.

2. Perfect safety now and for ever, for those who are in Christ; he is a fortress, high tower and city of refuge.

3. Marks of those who are in Christ.

In English I took Hosea 13:9.[115] Points were:

1. The people who were addressed.

2. What is said concerning them: 'Thou hast destroyed thyself.'

3. The remedy: 'In me is thine help.'

At 6pm I took Christ's preaching in Simon's boat and the massive 'draught of fishes'.

Sabbath 2nd June

Kilmorack. At noon Rev. Petros Mzamo[116] took Matthew 11:28.[117] He said that the yoke is meant for two to pull together. The sinner is yoked with his sins, both pulling towards a lost eternity. The saved sinner is yoked with grace and marching on towards everlasting life.

---

[115] 'O Israel, thou hast destroyed thyself; but in me is thine help.'

[116] Petros Mzamo (1918–2012) was a minister in the Free Presbyterian Church's Zimbabwe Presbytery. He pastored the Mbuma congregation—in which services were held in up to twelve locations—from 1962 until 2006. He translated (into the Ndebele language) the Westminster Shorter Catechism and helped complete the translation of the metrical Psalms. He also served as Moderator of Synod in 1963, the first man of colour to do so in a Scottish presbyterian denomination.

[117] 'Come unto me, all ye that labour and are heavy laden, and I will give you rest.'

Sabbath 28th July

Dingwall. I spoke in English from Genesis 24. Abraham gave Isaac all that he had. God the Father gave Christ all things. 'Of thy hands' works thou mad'st him Lord.'[118] In effectual calling, the Spirit shows the soul Christ's fulness.

Thursday 1st August

Dingwall communion. I have not seen so many strangers for many years as I saw today. Praise the Lord, this is what we have been praying for.

Friday 16th August

Bonar Bridge communion. The Question was in Luke 2:29–30. 'Lord, now lettest thou thy servant depart in peace, according to thy word: for mine eyes have seen thy salvation.' There were ten available to speak. My wife and I were at Badbea.[119]

---

[118] Psalm 8:6, metrical version.

[119] Badbea near Bonar Bridge was the family croft of the well-known theologian Professor John Murray (1898–1975). John Murray had been a divinity student of the Free Presbyterian Church and was sent to Princeton Theological Seminary, New Jersey, for further study. He was due to be licensed to preach by the FP Church in 1927 but this did not take place as he disagreed with the Synod's stance of barring from communion those who used public transport to attend church on the Lord's Day. After that he taught in the Theological Seminary in 1929 before being invited to join the faculty of the newly formed Westminster Theological Seminary, Pennsylvania, in 1930. He associated himself with the Free Church of Scotland after his return to Scotland in 1966 but often attended Free Presbyterian services. See Iain H. Murray, *Life of John Murray* in *Collected Writings of John Murray*. Vol. 3, *Life; Sermons; Reviews* (Edinburgh: Banner of Truth Trust, 1982), pp. 1–158.

Sabbath 25th August

Kilmorack. In the English I took Genesis 41:55–57. 'Go to Joseph.' Points:

1. There is a famine of the pure gospel in our day.
2. Our Lord Jesus Christ can supply all who will come to him. Pharaoh directed the people to Joseph. God directs all the spiritual Israel to his son Jesus Christ.
3. The key to the storehouse is faith and prayer.

Monday 26th August

My wife and I were at the prayer meeting in Inverness. We heard of the sudden death of John MacDonald, Oban.[120] Also we heard of the death of Alex Nicolson's wife in Glasgow.[121]

It becomes us to tremble for fear of God's judgments when the righteous are removed so frequently. Perhaps many of our churches will soon only have one service every Sabbath, or we will have none at all in some places. May the Lord build up Sion.

Friday 30th August

My wife and I visited James Cameron, Achterneed.[122] I believe he has the fear of God. After tea he made me sing in Gaelic in Psalm 34. He gave us some honey and apples.

---

[120] Mr MacDonald (1880–1957) used to cycle from Oban to Fort William on Saturdays, and back in the early hours of Monday morning, to supply Fort William, then doing a day's work. 'The late Mr John MacDonald, Elder, Oban', FPM Vol. 63 (June 1958): pp. 52–54.

[121] Alex and Katy (née Clark) Nicolson were well-known figures in the Glasgow congregation, in which he was an elder. He was from Raasay and she from Stoer. 'Obituary: Alexander Nicolson, Elder, Glasgow', FPM Vol. 75 (August 1970): pp. 131–135.

[122] Mr Cameron (c.1866–c.1964) became a divinity student in 1894 but was never ordained as a minister. Around 1900 he served as a

Sabbath 1st September

Dingwall. In Gaelic I took John 7:37 where Christ stood and cried, 'If any man thirst'.

In English I took Mount Sion in Hebrews 12:22.[123]

At 6.30 I took the virtuous woman of Proverbs 31. I applied the virtuous woman to the true church of Christ. The believer trades with the far country—his food is Christ in heaven. The believer's wisdom is from above, his strength is God alone. His affections are set on things above. His hope is in God's mercy.

Friday 6th September

Isabel Grant came on the No. 6 bus tonight with the recorder. I took as the basis of a few remarks 1 John 5:10. 'He that believeth on the Son of God hath the witness in himself.' Mrs Shaw and Rina, Moniack Bridge, were present. John came home from Gairloch and Ullapool.

Saturday 7th September

Mr Macfarlane and his wife are down at Hilton[124] for a fortnight; they left yesterday.

---

missionary in Strathpeffer and in 1905 in Tomatin. He later supplied Beauly and other congregations. Achterneed is close to Strathpeffer.

[123] 'But ye are come unto mount Sion, and unto the city of the living God, the heavenly Jerusalem, and to an innumerable company of angels.'

[124] The Macfarlanes stayed with Annie MacAngus in Hilton of Fearn, near Tain, on such occasions. Annie was noted for godliness and was the daughter of William MacAngus. 'The late Mr William MacAngus, elder, Fearn', *FPM* Vol. 44 (September 1939): pp. 183–187. Her sister Dolina was married to William Mackenzie (senior) of 'Deebank', Crown Drive, Inverness. The couple were well known for their hospitality and had four sons. Mr Mackenzie had two sisters—Eliza and Joey: the latter married Rev. William Grant, Halkirk.

Monday 9th September

Today is my birthday. I am 68. Many a time I verily thought I would not see so many years. I am only promised another two years but in one sense am not promised one day more. In a special manner when one reaches the allotted span he may expect the knock at the door with the summons. Of one thing I am certain, that I cannot make the crossing over Jordan without Christ. I pray daily that he be with me then. Dear reader, you cannot cross Jordan in your own strength, it is overflowing its banks for all who are Christless and will sweep them down to the Dead Sea of a lost eternity. May you and I then be daily in the exercise of faith, hope and love, and we shall see the other side safely.

Thursday 12th September

Prayer meeting, attendance was thirteen. I took Matthew 21:33, the parable of the householder.[125] I stressed the danger of living unfruitful lives under the gospel, and the awful consequences of it. It is only through union to Christ that we can become fruitful.

Saturday 14th September

My wife, John and I went to Aigas Home[126] at 3pm to keep a short service. There would be about a dozen present, mostly aged women approaching eternity. I took 1 John 3. I

---

[125] 'Hear another parable: There was a certain householder, which planted a vineyard, and hedged it round about, and digged a winepress in it, and built a tower, and let it out to husbandmen, and went into a far country.'

[126] Originally built for a tacksman (low-ranking landlord) in the 1760s, the house was a Council-run care home from the 1950s until 1971. It was subsequently redeveloped as a family home and field study centre.

stressed the necessity of being united to Christ before the end of our life comes.

Monday 16th September

I posted a letter to Mrs M today. I referred to assurance—knowing the law is the law and the gospel is the gospel, quoting Mr Macfarlane closing the Question. I referred to her husband's affliction as being a voice warning her that the old tabernacle was coming down, and that his heart would last long enough if it lasted God's time.

Thursday 19th September

John took the Kilmorack prayer meeting, attendance was fourteen.

My wife and I were in Dingwall as I had to take the service there. I took Song of Solomon 2:10. 'Rise up, my love, my fair one, and come away.' I remarked that these words may represent the general call of the gospel but that it is the elect alone who will hear and obey. It is by obeying the gospel that anyone shows he is of the elect, though he may indeed have doubts and fears himself. A mark of this people is that they are a praying people—not praying for life but because they have it.

Wednesday 25th September

We kept the Day of Prayer today at noon in Kilmorack. It was mainly a prayer meeting. Mr Macfarlane gave a short address from Isaiah 43:10. 'Ye are my witnesses.'

We had the evening service at 7pm in Dingwall. Mr Macfarlane gave a short address from the words in Colossians 1:27, 'Christ in you, the hope of glory'. In his address he said, 'If you are pleased with the terms of the covenant of grace, it is yours already.' How comforting!

Wednesday 2nd October

My wife and I went out collecting for a presentation to James Forbes as a token of our gratitude for his services to the Kilmorack congregation for 50 years. Mr Forbes has been very acceptable to the people, always willing and efficient. He rendered his services, looking for no praise or reward: a humble servant of God.

Sabbath 6th October

I was engaged at home today. In Gaelic (attendance was six). I took John 17:3. 'And this is life eternal, that they might know thee.'

In English I went through Exodus 35.

At 6pm I took Matthew 9:12. 'They that be whole need not a physician, but they that are sick.'

Sabbath 20th October

Kilmorack. In the Gaelic I took the transfiguration of Christ. When they lifted up their eyes they saw none but Jesus only.

In English I took Isaiah 51:1–4. The points I made were based on the words 'hearken to me' and 'following after righteousness' and 'seeking the Lord'.

At 6pm I took 1 Corinthians 1:30. 'But of him are ye in Christ Jesus, who of God is made unto us wisdom, and righteousness, and sanctification, and redemption.' Without wisdom from Christ, no one will discover that Christ is better than the world. No one without knowledge of what the law requires will value the righteousness of Christ.

Thursday 31st October

Mr Macfarlane was across today. I took the Gaelic service from Mark 4, Christ stilling the tempest. The points I made were:

1. We may meet with trouble and opposition.

2. He proved at once that he was human and divine: human in that he was asleep on a pillow, divine in that he arose and rebuked the wind and the sea.

3. He was in the right part of the ship, at the stern, the pilot's place. It will not do for us to just have the Word of God in our hands, in our houses, in our heads and in our memory; we must have it in our affections.

The minister preached from Romans 8:9, second sentence.[127]

At the prayer meeting I took Philippians 1:6.[128] The points I made regarding the 'good work' were:

1. It is not a work that one can do by the power of nature.

2. It is a work of God. It consists in illumination of the mind, bending of the will, and our affections raised from earth to heavenly things.

Sabbath 3rd November

Kilmorack. In the Gaelic I took Matthew 12:50 and the words 'he that doeth the will of God'.

In English I took the consecration of the priest in Leviticus 9 and referred to all believers being a spiritual priesthood.

At 6pm I took 'work out your own salvation' in Philippians 2:12. The only way mariners can 'work out' the position

---

[127] 'Now if any man have not the Spirit of Christ, he is none of his.'
[128] 'Being confident of this very thing, that he which hath begun a good work in you will perform it until the day of Jesus Christ.'

of the vessel on the high seas is by taking their bearings from the sun. The only way by which we can find our true position on the ocean of life is by finding out our relation to the sun of righteousness, Christ. 'What think ye of Christ?' will determine our fate for eternity.

Tuesday 5th November

My wife and I were at South Clunes giving James Forbes the presentation which consisted of a large Bible, psalmody and a wallet with money. He has rendered acceptable services as precentor to the Kilmorack congregation for fifty years. He asked me to convey his heartfelt wishes for such a token of their gratitude.

Thursday 7th November

We went to the Harvest Thanksgiving services in Dingwall. I took the Gaelic one, on Genesis 7, when Noah sacrificed on leaving the ark.

Mr Macfarlane took the English service from Ephesians 1:22–23, where Christ is spoken of as 'head over all things to the church'.

Tonight I took the prayer meeting in Beauly from Psalm 16:6. 'The lines are fallen unto me in pleasant places.' I spoke of the primary reference being to Canaan which was divided among the tribes. What a blessed people whose lines have fallen on the unchangeable, everlasting love of God! It is for ever and ever.

Sabbath 10th November

Dingwall. In Gaelic I took Matthew 16:18. 'Thou art Peter.'

In English, the cleansing of the leper in Leviticus 14.

At 6.30 I took Philippians 2:12. 'Work out your own salvation.' The points I made were:

1. Man is lost and needs salvation, the first step in recovery is to have a sense of one's lost state.

2. The manner in which working out one's salvation is to be carried out.

3. While our salvation is 'all of grace', God has promised to bestow it in the use of means.

4. The manner of working out: 'with fear and trembling'.

5. The encouragement given: 'It is God that worketh in you both to will and do' etc.

Thursday 14th November

Beauly Harvest Thanksgiving services. We had services the same as Sabbath.[129] I took Psalm 105:1. 'Give thanks to God, call on his name.' I said that we require three things for gratitude:

1. A sense of our deserts.

2. That we know the value of the blessings bestowed.

3. That we love the giver.

Rev. D.A. Macfarlane preached from Acts 14:7. 'And there they preached the gospel.' He said that one example of that was Paul himself. The gospel changed him from a lion into a lamb. Through the gospel of Christ Paul found pardon for his crimson sins.

At 7pm I took the grain of wheat in John 12.

Sabbath 17th November

Kilmorack. In Gaelic, Psalm 48:12 'Walk about Zion, and go round about her: tell the towers thereof.' I made Zion to

---

[129] Meaning at the same times as the Sabbath services.

be the gospel church and individual believers. The high towers were the attributes of God, pledged to preserve her.

In English I took their 'being of one accord in the temple' from Acts 2:46. I made some observations on the feast of Pentecost. It was partly to commemorate the giving of the law at Sinai amidst terrors. At Pentecost in the book of Acts, the gospel law went forth, and converted three thousand people at once.

At 6pm I took 1 Timothy 4:12.[130]

Thursday 28th November

Tonight I took the phrase 'the day shall declare it' in 1 Corinthians 3:13. I applied it to the day of judgment when all the secrets of men's hearts shall be revealed—their intentions, motives, spirits and temper. I referred to the Term Day (when men are asked to settle their accounts, pay their rent)[131] and that it should suggest to us our removal from time to eternity, which may be any day. We should endeavour to make sure of another house. Dear reader, make sure work of being in Christ.

Sabbath 1st December

I took the services at home today. Six attended the Gaelic, where I took the seed that fell on good ground in Luke 8.

In English my text was Leviticus 25:10. 'And ye shall hallow the fiftieth year.' I made some remarks on the Jubilee.

---

[130] 'Let no man despise thy youth; but be thou an example of the believers, in word, in conversation, in charity, in spirit, in faith, in purity.'
[131] Term days were traditionally the dates when rents were due and on which contracts and leases began and ended. There were four in Scotland: Candlemas (2nd February), Whitsunday (15th May), Lammas (1st August) and Martinmas (11th November).

The gospel is the New Testament trumpet of Jubilee, proclaiming liberty to all who are slaves of Satan and serving diverse lusts and pleasures, the gospel declaring to them that they can have restored to them what they lost in the fall: the love and favour of a triune God.

At 6pm I took parts of Titus 1:3, and dwelt mainly on the greatness of God's mercy manifested in the salvation of lost sinners.

Monday 9th December

John and I attended the funeral of M today. He was in his 97th year. I believe he went to the 'better country'. He was saying in his last days on earth: 'Two things I regret and I am too late now—I never spoke to the Question on Friday and I never went to the Lord's Table.' May that be a warning to others.

Sabbath 15th December

Kilmorack. At 6pm I took Numbers 9 and the command to keep the Passover. I spoke of the great danger of despising the solemn ordinance, as in the chapter where it says that the person not on a journey, but who forbears to keep the Passover, shall be cut off.

Wednesday 25th December

We spent the day at home. We could have a 'Xmas' every day if rightly exercised.[132] We could daily say, 'O sing a new

---

[132] Alex reflected the position of the Free Presbyterian Church that Christ's incarnation and resurrection should be a daily source of worship and should not be observed on man-made special days. In common with the Reformers and Puritans, the Church opposes the celebration of 'festivals' such as 'Christmas' as these are not commanded in the Bible.

song to the Lord, for wonders he hath done.' The enemy is coming in like a flood. Popery is gaining ground rapidly in our beloved land. I am only afraid we are ripening for the vials of God's wrath. Our land is steeped in Popery, pleasure-seeking and false worship. The true Christian cannot but feel sore over it. Our prime minister attending mass:[133] we never expected to see such a day. May God's judgment be averted by a speedy repentance.

Thursday 26th December

My wife and I attended the marriage ceremony of Rev. D.M. Macleod[134] at Inverness church. There was a large gathering. Rev. D.A. Macfarlane officiated. Rev. R.R. Sinclair sang.[135] Rev. A.F. Mackay prayed in conclusion.

---

[133] Harold Macmillan (1894–1986) was Prime Minister from January 1957 until October 1963. In August 1957 he attended a requiem mass for his friend Ronald Knox (1888–1957), a Roman Catholic priest and former Anglican chaplain of Trinity College, Oxford.

[134] Donald Malcolm Macleod (1920–1978) married Shona Fraser of Redcastle. He was minister in Lairg and Bonar from 1956 to 1961, then in Stornoway from 1961 to 1968, with a final charge in Auckland, New Zealand, from 1968 until his death. He was editor of *The Young People's Magazine* from 1957 to 1968. 'Obituary: The late Reverend Donald Malcolm Macleod', *FPM* Vol. 85 (August 1980): pp. 246–50.

[135] Robert Ross Sinclair (1898–1997) was born at Pulteneytown, Wick. He was a son of Rev. J.S. Sinclair (1867–1921), the minister of the John Knox congregation in Glasgow from 1896 until his death in 1921. Rev. R.R. Sinclair served as the assistant minister at Glasgow's larger FP congregation, St Jude's, from 1928 until 1931. He then returned to Wick, whose FP congregation he served from 1931 until 1989. He was Clerk of Synod for forty-two years and edited the *Free Presbyterian Magazine* for twenty years, from 1949 to 1969. Mr Sinclair joined the Associated Presbyterian Churches (APC) in 1989.

We then visited in the Northern Infirmary. I saw Mr M. He has an obstruction in his throat. I tried to put the way of salvation before him. He appeared to be somewhat moved. He said that people might learn to speak of the blood of Christ (which was very true). I told him the test was, do we really feel our need of being washed?

Sabbath 29th December

Kilmorack. In Gaelic I took Mark 3:35. 'Whosoever shall do the will of God, the same is my brother, and my sister, and mother.'

In English I took Luke 14:22. 'Yet there is room.' The points I made were:

1. The supper of the gospel.
2. There is room for all who will come.
3. The time will come when there will be no room.
4. The danger and folly of delaying our repentance.

At 6pm I took the 'tidings of great joy' in Luke 2:10. I spoke of the joyful sound of the Jubilee trumpet and that the gospel is a joyful sound to those who are poor, oppressed by the devil, serving diverse lusts and pleasures.

1958

Wednesday 1st January

Kilmorack, New Year's Day service. 2 Corinthians 5:17. 'If any man be in Christ, he is a new creature.'

Sabbath 5th January

I took the services in Dingwall today. In Gaelic I took Joshua 24:15.[136]

In English I took John 3:3.[137]

At 6.30pm my text was Psalm 86:11.[138] I made four points.

1. The teacher.
2. The scholar.
3. The lesson.
4. The walk.

---

[136] 'And if it seem evil unto you to serve the Lord, choose you this day whom ye will serve; whether the gods which your fathers served that were on the other side of the flood, or the gods of the Amorites, in whose land ye dwell: but as for me and my house, we will serve the Lord.'

[137] 'Jesus answered and said unto him, Verily, verily, I say unto thee, Except a man be born again, he cannot see the kingdom of God.'

[138] 'Teach me thy way, O Lord; I will walk in thy truth: unite my heart to fear thy name.'

1959

Thursday 1st January

We had a service at noon today. I read a portion in Ezekiel 36 and spoke a little on the new heart. I observed that:

1. The old heart is condemned, deceitful and wicked, a workshop of Satan out of which proceeds all manner of evil words and deeds.

2. The new heart is God's workmanship.

3. We must believe God's promise, that he can and will give it.

4. We must sincerely seek it.

5. The properties of the new heart: it aims at God's glory, God's law is written on it, it seeks the prosperity and peace of Christ's kingdom.

Friday 2nd January

I was reading this morning where Rehoboam refused the counsel of the old men and took the young men's counsel. One would think that common sense would suggest a better course to him. Love and goodwill are the most powerful weapons to conquer and disarm those who differ from and oppose us. The Bible says, 'Let all your things be done in love,' even in rebuking sin in our fellows, which is hard at times. It must be done according to Scripture rules. The flesh must be subdued. When the passions are out of control they resemble a chariot in which the devil drives, so let us beware.

Thursday 8th January

Snow and frost. Kilmorack prayer meeting, attendance was ten. I spoke of the rich young man who came to Christ (Matthew 19) and observed some points on which he was in error.

1. He appeared to have wrong or defective views of Christ's person, as the Saviour's answer shows.

2. He did not know the spirituality of the law, its extensive compass.

3. He had an excessive love of the world.

4. He did not believe what Christ was promising if he would follow him.

5. He did not care for the poor as he was commanded by Christ.

Sabbath 11th January

Snow and frost. One service in Kilmorack. In Gaelic I took John 13.

In English I took Micah 4:2.[139] My points were:

1. The narrow ways.

2. The ways of peace.

3. The way of holiness.

I also spoke of the mountain. It is the work of God; it is high above the common level; it is the emblem of stability,

---

[139] 'And many nations shall come, and say, Come, and let us go up to the mountain of the Lord, and to the house of the God of Jacob; and he will teach us of his ways, and we will walk in his paths: for the law shall go forth of Zion, and the word of the Lord from Jerusalem.'

perpetuity and antiquity; one can see afar from its summit. I applied this to the true church of God, Mount Zion.

Monday 12ᵗʰ January

I was reading today in 2 Chronicles 18 and 19 where Ahab and Jehoshaphat helped each other in war. The latter was rebuked by the prophet. We should form no connection with the enemies of God. Jehoshaphat seems to have had the fear of God. He put away idolatry, reformed Judah and said to the priests and judges to 'deal courageously'.

Friday 23ʳᵈ January

Inverness communion, Question Meeting. The Question was given out by Robert Watt. John 16:33. 'These things I have spoken unto you, that in me ye might have peace. In the world ye shall have tribulation: but be of good cheer; I have overcome the world.' He asked for marks of those who have this peace and this tribulation. About six spoke.

Saturday 31ˢᵗ January

J came forward in full membership. When asked for his experience, he said it started when he was in France in the First World War. He also said there was no company he desired but the people of God. Rev. Colquhoun[140] gave him a very earnest exhortation as to how he should endeavour to live to the glory of God, and adorn his profession.

---

[140] John Colquhoun (1896–1976) was minister of Glendale from 1933 until 1974. 'Rev. John Colquhoun, Glendale', *FPM* Vol. 83 (August 1978): pp. 214–218.

Sabbath 1st February

Rev. Colquhoun preached in Gaelic and English from Song of Solomon 7:5. 'The king is held in the galleries.' In the Gaelic he mainly spoke on the King.

At 12 noon in English he spoke mainly of the galleries. These are the gallery of God's Word, the gallery of the preaching of the gospel, and the gallery of the sacraments of the Lord's Supper and baptism.

Thursday 5th February

I took the Kilmorack prayer meeting. 1 Peter 2:7.[141] The late Rev. Macfarlane said, 'Faith is the breadwinner. Where he is sick, the family will not be well off.'

Thursday 19th February

John took the Kilmorack prayer meeting as I was not fit because of my shoulder. Proverbs 8:34.[142] Eliza said he had unusual liberty. Attendance nineteen.

Sabbath 1st March

Dingwall. In the English I took the Gentile centurion in Luke 7. The main points were: his sympathy and concern for his servant; his faith; his humility; his views of himself; his views of Christ; his success. He got what he desired, and Christ's commendation.

---

[141] 'Unto you therefore which believe he is precious: but unto them which be disobedient, the stone which the builders disallowed, the same is made the head of the corner.'
[142] 'Blessed is the man that heareth me, watching daily at my gates, waiting at the posts of my doors.'

Thursday 5th March

Kilmorack prayer meeting. I spoke from the parable of the good Samaritan in Luke 10, about the man going from Jerusalem to Jericho and 'fell among thieves'. Mankind left the state of holiness and descended into the state of the curse. The ceremonial law cannot help him. The moral law cannot help him. Christ finds the sinner and helps him, healing him with his word.

Thursday 12th March

Attendance eleven. I took as my text tonight John 6:37. 'All that the Father giveth me shall come to me; and him that cometh to me I will in no wise cast out.' Some remarks I made: we are commanded to come; we cannot come; if we don't come we cannot be saved; God can empower us to come willingly unto him; it is our duty to seek this, it is at our peril we neglect it.

Monday 16th March

I was in Raigmore Hospital today for an X-ray of my shoulder, the only time I have been admitted to hospital in my life, with the exception of when I had the flu in New Zealand during World War One. I am in my 70th year. How I should praise God that at my age I do not feel any trace of disease, only a lessening of physical energy.

Saturday 28th March

D. Mackenzie, Chapelton,[143] came in with news of the death of Rev. James Fraser of the African Mission.[144] What a

---

[143] Donald Mackenzie and his wife Ina lived on Chapelton farm on the outskirts of Muir of Ord. It should not be confused with the nearby Chapelton, Killearnan, birthplace of Lachlan Mackenzie (1754–1819), the minister of Lochcarron from 1782 until his death.

shock it gave us! However, it was the will of God and we believe he went to the better country. His work was finished.

Friday 10th April

Donald Beaton, Balnabeen,[145] and I went to Dingwall today, and along with Dugald Matheson[146] were attending to minor details of finishing touches to the new church which is to be opened Tuesday 12th May at 7pm, DV.

Wednesday 29th April

Attendance of seventeen at the prayer meeting. I took Acts 5:42. 'And daily in the temple, and in every house, they ceased not to teach and preach Jesus Christ.' The main points in preaching Jesus Christ are: the dignity of his person; his obedience; his death; the efficacy of his blood.

Tuesday 12th May

The new church at Dingwall was officially opened this evening.[147]

---

[144] James S. Fraser (1913–1959) from Strathpeffer served as a well-loved missionary in Southern Rhodesia (now Zimbabwe) from 1947 until 1959. For an account of his life, see Alexander McPherson, *James Fraser: A record of missionary endeavour in Rhodesia in the twentieth century* (London: Banner of Truth Trust, 1967).

[145] Popularly known as 'Wallace Beaton', a civil engineer from Lochcarron who later spent some years in Auckland where he helped build the Free Presbyterian church. Balnabeen is in the Black Isle.

[146] Mr Matheson worked in a Dingwall solicitor's office and was helpful in the administrative side of congregational life. He provided much hospitality at communion seasons.

[147] Over four hundred attended this service. The preacher was Rev. William Grant, Halkirk. His text was Jude 1:3: 'Beloved, when I gave all diligence to write unto you of the common salvation, it was needful for me to write unto you, and exhort you that ye should earnestly contend for the faith which was once delivered unto the

Saturday 16th May

Halkirk. I visited A at H. He was very lively and talked of many things. He is supposed to be mentally weak, but in spiritual conversation I felt it was I who was weak-minded, not him. He was speaking about fallen man being worse than devils, having a heart 'deceitful above all things'.

Sabbath 24th May

I was preaching for the first time in the new church in Dingwall. In the morning English service, I took 2 Corinthians 5:17. 'If any man be in Christ, he is a new creature.' I asked: 'What will a new church do for us at last without a new creation?'

Thursday 27th August

Prayer meeting attendance: thirteen. After I started the service tonight, I noticed Rev. Fraser MacDonald, Tolsta, had come in, so after the first prayer I invited him to address the meeting.[148] He took his text from Mark 12:34, 'Thou art not far from the kingdom of God.' He stressed the sting it would be to a soul to come to the gate of heaven only to find it shut against him.

Sabbath 6th September

Kilmorack. In English I took John 6:68. 'Lord, to whom shall we go? thou hast the words of eternal life.' I observed

---

saints.' An 'overflow' service was led by Rev. R.R. Sinclair in the old church. 'New Church opened in Dingwall', *FPM* Vol. 64 (July 1959): pp. 81–82.

[148] Rev. Fraser MacDonald (1924–2013) was much influenced by Rev. D.A. Macfarlane of Dingwall. He served as pastor of North Tolsta from 1952 until 1966 and then in Portree (Isle of Skye) from 1966 until he retired in 2006. 'Rev. Fraser Macdonald', *FPM* Vol. 118 (November 2013): pp. 342–344.

that although Peter and the other disciples were hazy about some aspects of the work of the Lord at this time, he was never in doubt about Christ's person. He was convinced of his divinity and so must we be.

Thursday 10th September

Kilmorack prayer meeting, the attendance was 19. I took Psalm 40:1–4. I spoke of the 'fearful pit' and that some people might say they had never found themselves in a fearful pit. Well, if you have gone deep enough to know that only Christ can take you out of it, why should you wish to go deeper? You should rather praise God if he has brought you to the knowledge of Christ in an easier way than others.

Thursday 17th September

Kilmorack prayer meeting, attendance ten. I spoke of the parable of the two debtors in Luke 7:37–50. The creditor is God. The debtors are the lost race of Adam going deeper into debt with every breath we draw. All alike have nothing to pay their debts, neither the moral men nor notorious sinners. God is willing to forgive us on the ground of the atoning sacrifice of Christ.

Thursday 8th October

Kilmorack prayer meeting, attendance was eight. I took 1 Peter 1:18, particularly 'Forasmuch as ye know that ye were not redeemed with corruptible things as silver and gold'. The points I made were:

1. The people redeemed had previously been lost and in a state of nature, under the curse, and in bondage to sin and Satan.

2. What it cost to redeem them—the blood of Christ.

3. What the conduct of such ought to be—to glorify God with soul, body and spirit.

Thursday 15th October

Day of Prayer. Rev. D.A. Macfarlane preached at Kilmorack today from Elijah on Carmel. He said that Israel was guilty in four outstanding things:

1. They despised the promise given them of Christ who was to come.

2. They despised the righteousness which is by faith in him.

3. They neglected personal holiness and works of faith and love.

4. They despised the city which hath foundations, which Abraham looked for.

At 7pm in Dingwall, Mr Macfarlane preached a little on 1 Timothy 3:16. 'Great is the mystery of godliness: God was manifest in the flesh.' He said it needed the teaching of heaven before any could savingly accept the inspiration of the Bible from Genesis to Revelation. Those praying were John, Mr Kelly, James Forbes and myself.

Thursday 29th October

I once heard a man praying who was not quite at home in English but his theology was good. He said in prayer: 'The flesh has a good part of our hearts. We have cause to fear we are often in the flesh when we should be at the feet of Christ.'

We had three services in Kilmorack today.

At 7pm I took 1 John 1:8. 'If we say that we have no sin, we deceive ourselves, and the truth is not in us.' I spoke of four steps which believers experience in greater or lesser degree:

1. To know their sins.
2. To confess them.
3. To forsake them.
4. To hate sin—this is the most difficult step.

Thursday 5th November

Thanksgiving Day, Dingwall. Mr Macfarlane preached twice: in Gaelic in Deuteronomy 16:16[149] and in English in 2 Corinthians 9:15.[150]

I had to take the evening service. Psalm 105:1–2. 'Give thanks to God, call on his name' etc. I observed three things we must have before we are really thankful:

1. We must have a sense of our deserts.
2. We must value what is done for us.
3. We will desire to honour and serve the giver.

Friday 6th November

I left for Halkirk about noon. The Question Meeting was put off until tonight. It was given out by James Davidson,[151] it was Malachi 3:16. 'Then they that feared the Lord spake often

---

[149] 'Three times in a year shall all thy males appear before the Lord thy God in the place which he shall choose; in the feast of unleavened bread, and in the feast of weeks, and in the feast of tabernacles: and they shall not appear before the Lord empty.'

[150] 'Thanks be unto God for his unspeakable gift.'

[151] James Davidson was a 'loved and respected' elder in the Halkirk-Helmsdale congregation. He died in September 1971. His brother and fellow elder there, Alec John, outlived him by six years. 'The Late Mr James Davidson, Helmsdale', *FPM* Vol. 77 (May 1972): pp. 153–155. See also 'Tribute to the late Mr James Davidson, Elder, Helmsdale', *Synod Proceedings, May 1972* (Glasgow, 1972), pp. 31–32.

one to another.' There were three to speak, Rev. William Grant included.[152]

Thursday 26th November

I took Matthew 1:21. 'He shall save his people from their sins.' The points I made were:

1. We must discover we are lost.
2. We must see that Christ is an all-sufficient Saviour.
3. We must apply for it by faith and prayer.
4. If we do not believe Christ, we will die in our sins.

Monday 30th November

I visited Murdo Campbell, Inverness[153] who is apparently dying. I asked him if he had anything to say. He replied, 'I have been for long praying that I might die as a little child. I have now got my wish fulfilled to the very letter. They are doing everything for me, but I hope I meant it in a higher sense than that.' He also said, 'My hope is in his word.' So, I bade him goodbye after praying, likely never to see him on earth again.

Tuesday 8th December

I attended Murdo Campbell's funeral, which was large. Rev. Sinclair prayed first, Mr Grant finished. Mr Mackay read

---

[152] Rev. William Grant (1886–1976) was born in Dornoch. Ordained and inducted on 29th June 1926 to the joint charge of Halkirk and Helmsdale, he died in 1976 after a ministry which was well known across the northern counties of Scotland. Margaret Campbell, *Rev. William Grant* (Inverness: n.p., 1978); 'Obituary: Rev. William Grant, Halkirk', *FPM* Vol. 83 (February 1978): pp. 49–54.

[153] Mr Campbell (1883–1959) was an elder in the Inverness Free Presbyterian congregation. He came from Strathy and was noted for his humility. 'Mr Murdo Campbell, Elder, Inverness', *FPM* Vol. 67 (February 1963): pp. 305–308.

in 1 Corinthians 15. Murdo Campbell was a 'lily of the valleys'. His departure is a loss to the world, but his gain.

Thursday 10th December

Tonight I took Proverbs 18:10. 'The name of the Lord is a strong tower, the righteous runneth into it and is safe.' Points:

1. The enemies from which we need defence.
2. The manner in which the name of the Lord is a defence.
3. The people mentioned in the text—the righteous.
4. Their exercise—running. We must strive to enter in. As Bunyan said, 'He that will go to heaven must run for it.'[154]

Sabbath 20th December

Kilmorack. This is the last of the Gaelic in this place in the meantime. In the Gaelic I took Revelation 22:14. 'Blessed are they that do his commandments, that they may have right to the tree of life, and may enter in through the gates into the city.'

In English I took Psalm 92:12. 'The righteous shall flourish like the palm tree.' I observed that the palm tree is an evergreen; the more weight put upon it the more it grows; it affords shade and nourishment to the weary traveller; it bears fruit until old age; if anything injures its head, it remains barren.

Thursday 24th December

Kilmorack prayer meeting, the attendance was eleven. I took Luke 24:29. 'But they constrained him, saying, Abide

---

[154] A quotation from *The Heavenly Footman*.

with us: for it is toward evening, and the day is far spent. And he went in to tarry with them.' The points I made were:

1. We are drawing near eternity.

2. Our day is far spent; we should constrain Christ.

3. Christ will come in to those who seek him with all their heart.

4. He will give them meat to eat that the world knows nothing about.

Sabbath 27th December

I took the words 'Glory to God in the highest' from Luke 2:14. Points:

1. We have ceased to give glory to God by the fall in Eden.

2. Christ came and glorified God by becoming incarnate.

3. Marks of those who glorify God.

1960

Thursday 7th January

Kilmorack prayer meeting, twenty-one present. Tonight I took 2 John verse 9. 'He that abideth in the doctrine of Christ, he hath both the Father and the Son.' The doctrine of Christ included:

1. Total ruin by the fall.
2. That Christ is the only Saviour.
3. Repentance towards God, faith, justification, sanctification, through the work of the Spirit.

Friday 8th January

Today Rev. Archibald Beaton,[155] Gairloch was buried. We heard there were about a thousand people at the funeral.

---

[155] Archibald Beaton (1900–1960) was from Skye. After service in the Merchant Navy, he was accepted as a divinity student and was inducted to the Gairloch congregation in 1933. He remained in that charge until his death. Mr Beaton was known for his close study of the English Puritans. The Synod tribute records: 'In the homes of the sick and afflicted he was a welcome visitor because of his known piety and large-hearted sympathy.' 'To Rev. A. Beaton, Gairloch', *Synod Proceedings, May 1960* (Glasgow, 1960): pp. 30–31; 'The

Sabbath 10th January

Beauly 6pm. Mark 3:35. 'For whosoever shall do the will of God, the same is my brother, and my sister, and mother.' All the animate and inanimate creation fulfils the end for which they were made but man (created originally in the image of God) is the only rebel on this earth. I spoke a little of the great privilege of having God so near to us as brothers, sisters and a mother—as all true believers in Christ can claim.

Tuesday 12th January

We had a call from Mr and Mrs Macfarlane in the afternoon: we heard that Rev. James Tallach, Stornoway died, only 64.[156] What a loud voice to us!

Wednesday 13th January

We went to the induction of Rev. D.J. Matheson, Glasgow,[157] over the joint charge of Stratherrick-Tomatin-Daviot. Rev. D.M. Macleod preached from Philippians 2:14–16.[158]

Late Rev. Archibald Beaton, Gairloch', *FPM* Vol. 66 (August 1961): pp. 114–118.

[156] James Andrew Tallach (1896–1960) served in Canada, London, Kames and Stornoway. Notes by hearers of his preaching, *Sermons and Meditations*, were published in 1962 (Dingwall: n.p.) and republished in 1978. 'The Late Rev. James A. Tallach, Stornoway', *FPM* Vol. 65 (March 1961): pp. 337–342.

[157] Mr Matheson (1890–1962) belonged to Harris. He was minister of Lairg from 1926 until 1946 and then of St Jude's, Glasgow, from 1946 until 1960. From then until his death he was pastor of the Daviot-Stratherrick-Tomatin joint charge. 'Rev. Donald John Matheson, Errogie', *FPM* Vol. 67 (March 1963): pp. 335–338.

[158] 'Do all things without murmurings and disputings: that ye may be blameless and harmless, the sons of God, without rebuke, in the midst of a crooked and perverse nation, among whom ye shine as lights in the world; holding forth the word of life; that I may rejoice

Sabbath 17ᵗʰ January

Beauly. At noon I took Mark 5:25[159] on the woman with the issue of blood. The points made were:

1. Sin is the cause of all maladies.

2. We are prone to look to the creature.

3. We forget that Christ is the procuring cause of all our mercies.

4. The woman heard of Jesus.

In Dingwall at 6.30 my text was Isaiah 57:1–2. 'The righteous perisheth' etc.

1. God speaks in his providence

2. The stupidity of men in taking no notice.

3. It is a bad sign when the ambassadors are called home.

Friday 29ᵗʰ January

Inverness communion, Question Meeting. The text was given out by Robert Watt[160] in 1 Peter 2:3. 'If so be ye have tasted that the Lord is gracious.' Sixteen rose to speak.

One thing can be safely said about the Question, that all who are born again get a good taste from the pure gospel and get a bad taste from what is not the gospel.

Friday 5ᵗʰ February

Dingwall communion. The Question was given out by John Maclennan in Titus 3:5. 'Not by works of righteousness which we have done, but according to his mercy he saved us, by the washing of regeneration, and renewing of the Holy Ghost.' About ten spoke. It was opened by Mr Mackay

---

in the day of Christ, that I have not run in vain, neither laboured in vain.'

[159] 'And a certain woman, which had an issue of blood twelve years.'

[160] Robert Watt or Finlay Beaton were the elders most likely to suggest a text on such occasions in Inverness.

(Inverness). It was closed by Mr Macfarlane, who said, 'We should praise God that we have such a day yet, when other churches don't have a fellowship meeting at all in some quarters.'

Sabbath 7th February

Inverness communion. At the evening service, Mr MacAskill, Lochinver,[161] preached from Revelation 3:20.[162] I thought it was very solemn.

Monday 8th February

Rev. MacAskill preached from Psalm 84:11. 'For the Lord God is a sun and shield.' He pointed out that the sun rules in the earth and over it, is the source of power, light, growth and fruitfulness. Rev. Mackay preached from Isaiah 14:32.[163]

Thursday 18th February

Kilmorack prayer meeting, fifteen attended. We had the two divinity students tonight. Mr McPherson[164] gave a

---

[161] Mr MacAskill was born and raised in North Uist. He served in the Army in the First World War, and later worked in Fort William. He was ordained and inducted as pastor of Assynt in 1937, where he served for over 40 years. He was frequently a visiting minister at communion seasons. 'The late Rev. Alexander MacAskill, Lochinver', *FPM* Vol. 89 (May 1984): pp. 150–154.

[162] 'Behold, I stand at the door, and knock: if any man hear my voice, and open the door, I will come in to him, and will sup with him, and he with me.'

[163] 'What shall one then answer the messengers of the nation? That the Lord hath founded Zion, and the poor of his people shall trust in it.'

[164] See footnote 68.

discourse from 1 Corinthians 15:19.[165] He spoke of several causes of men's misery.

1. A feeling of shame and guilt for sin.

2. A growing awareness of the cause of all these evils being within.

3. Mourning for an absent Christ, desiring to taste again what they once tasted.

4. Their loneliness increases because they are in an alien country.

5. Their concern for others' safety.

6. Their concern for Christ's cause.

Sabbath 13th March

In Dingwall at the English I took 2 Thessalonians 2:13.[166] Sanctification: God is the author of it, the sustainer of it, the restorer of it, the finisher of it.

At Beauly at 6pm I took the words 'Enter thou into thy chambers' from Isaiah 26:20. I mentioned that Noah entered into the ark and also mentioned Israel in Egypt and the destroying angel. Rahab in Jericho was safe in her house with the scarlet thread hung from the window. The chambers the Lord's people enter into are the chambers of omnipotence, omniscience, omnipresence, infinite wisdom, his everlasting love, the chamber of election, and all the attributes of God.

---

[165] 'If in this life only we have hope in Christ, we are of all men most miserable.'

[166] 'But we are bound to give thanks alway to God for you, brethren beloved of the Lord, because God hath from the beginning chosen you to salvation through sanctification of the Spirit and belief of the truth.'

Sabbath 20th March

At Dingwall at 6.30 I took Acts 3:22. 'A prophet shall the Lord your God raise up unto you of your brethren, like unto me.' I touched on points of similarity between Moses and Christ. Moses was a lawgiver, he was a mediator; he took Israel out of Egypt, he revealed to Israel the mind of God.

Thursday 7th April

Diabeg.[167] I was at John Maclennan's funeral. I kept the prayer meeting in his house after we put him in the coffin; the attendance was twenty. I spoke on 'all the counsel of God' from Acts 20:27. His counsel consists in: total ruin by the fall, regeneration by the Holy Spirit, redemption by Jesus Christ.

Tuesday 19th April

We passed a pleasant evening at the Urquharts in Resolis. I read in the Song of Solomon 2:11. 'For, lo, the winter is past, the rain is over and gone.' I applied it to the soul arising from its natural state at the time of effectual calling. The marks of winter are that the sun is far off, the ground is hard, and the shadows are large. The marks of summer are that the earth turns towards the sun, soft winds blow, the shadows grow small, flowers appear, and the voice of the turtle dove is heard.

Wednesday 20th April

I was at A's funeral. There were many wreaths. A man said to me, 'There are only two flowers I want myself, the rose of Sharon and the lily of the valleys.' It was a beautiful thought.

---

[167] Now known as Diabaig.

Sabbath 22nd May

Dingwall. At 6.30 I took the account of Christ sending the disciples for the loan of an ass. I made some observations. The ass suggests to us man in his unregenerate state. The ass tied is like man bound by Satan who cannot move his head or feet. The disciples were to find the colt straight ahead—the unregenerate are found everywhere. We should consider it the highest honour that Christ would ask anything of us.

Thursday 26th May

Prayer meeting, thirteen attended. I took John 6:40.[168] We cannot see the sun (Christ) any sooner by education, intellect or example until he will reveal himself in us, no more than we can see the literal sun any sooner by the help of artificial light. Those who see him will believe in him.

Friday 10th June

Shieldaig communion. The Question was given out by D. Mackenzie, Shieldaig, in 1 Peter 1:23. 'Being born again, not of corruptible seed, but of incorruptible, by the word of God, which liveth and abideth for ever.' There would be about ten to speak.

There was a service in Ardheslaig[169] in the evening.

Sabbath 12th June

Shieldaig communion. Rev. A.F. Mackay preached the Action Sermon[170] in Gaelic from Isaiah 53:6. 'All we like

---

[168] 'And this is the will of him that sent me, that every one which seeth the Son, and believeth on him, may have everlasting life: and I will raise him up at the last day.'

[169] A crofting settlement on the southern shore of Loch Torridon, about 3 miles (5 km) from Shieldaig.

sheep have gone astray; we have turned every one to his own way; and the Lord hath laid on him the iniquity of us all.' I thought he had great liberty.

Monday 13th June

At the close of the communion I was working to help build the sea wall at Tighnamara.[171] I had Charlie Macleod, Raasay,[172] with me. God is spoken of in Scripture regarding his power as one who sets bound to the sea that it cannot pass over it though its waves toss and roar. How little we think of this when the sea is at our doorstep!

Saturday 2nd July

We had a new member in Beauly today. A man came forward,[173] weeping. What a rare sight in this degenerate age!

---

[170] The Westminster Assembly's *Directory for the Publick Worship of God* (1645) contains a section entitled *Of the celebration of the communion, or sacrament of the Lord's supper*. After preaching, prayer and exhortation, 'the minister is to begin the action with sanctifying and blessing the elements of bread and wine'. This may account for the term 'Action Sermon' being applied to the sermon. The phrase appears to have originated in the late seventeenth century.

[171] The name means 'House of the sea' in Gaelic.

[172] Most likely Charlie Macleod of Arnish, Rassay (1929–2012), who moved to Portree in the late 1960s and later wrote a book about Rona: *South Rona: The island and its people*, ed. Rebecca Mackay, (Raasay: Raasay Heritage Trust, 2016). Charlie's brother Calum stayed on in Arnish and single-handedly built a road to the settlement. See Roger Hutchinson, *Calum's Road* (Edinburgh: Birlinn, 2006).

[173] An expression used in churches for attending the Kirk Session to make a public profession and thereafter take communion for the first time.

Friday 8th July

Tain communion. The Question was given out by George Murray.[174] 1 Chronicles 4:10. 'And Jabez called on the God of Israel, saying, Oh that thou wouldest bless me indeed, and enlarge my coast, and that thine hand might be with me, and that thou wouldest keep me from evil, that it may not grieve me! And God granted him that which he requested.' I don't remember ever feeling it so easy for me to speak. It seemed to open up for me right away: the Question expressed my own experience.

Wednesday 20th July

My wife arrived home from Lochinver where she has been for ten days. Praise the Lord for his care. 'Thy going out and coming in, God keep for ever will.' All united to Christ have the warrant of Scripture to plead that precious promise. He took care of us coming into the world. He will as surely take care of them going out, who trust in him and look to Jesus.

Sabbath 24th July

Beauly evening service. I took 1 Corinthians 1:30–31. I made some remarks on wisdom, righteousness, sanctification and redemption. We had a minister from Holland, a Mr Tukker,[175] who prayed.

---

[174] Mr Murray (1883–1964) was father of Rev. Alexander Murray and brother of Prof. John Murray, Westminster Theological Seminary. 'The late George Murray, Elder, Bonar Bridge and Lairg', *FPM* Vol. 71 (July 1966): pp. 85–87.

[175] W.L. Tukker (1908–1988) was a minister in the Nederlandse Hervormde Kerk (Dutch Reformed Church) and a leading member in the Gereformeerde Bond (Reformed Association), a conservative grouping within that denomination. He held pastorates at various locations in the Netherlands and at this juncture was minister of Katwijk aan Zee, a fishing port on the North Sea coast. He visited

Sabbath 31st July

Dingwall. I got J. Mackenzie[176] to take the 6.30 service. He took the 'feast of fat things' from Isaiah 25:6. He took the feast to mean Christ's divinity, humanity, crucifixion, resurrection, ascension and intercession.

Friday 5th August

Dingwall communion. The Question was given by John Maclennan, Muir of Ord, in Numbers 14:24.[177] Marks were asked of those who have 'another spirit' to distinguish them from those who have the spirit of the world. Nine or ten spoke.

Friday 19th August

Bonar Bridge communion. The Question was given out by George Murray in Colossians 3:2. 'Set your affection on things above, not on things on the earth.' He wanted marks of those whose affections were not [sic] on things above. About eight spoke or were called. I was for dinner with Professor John Murray at Badbea.

Thursday 1st September

I took the meeting in Dingwall as the minister is away. The text was Acts 28:24. 'And some believed the things which were spoken, and some believed not.' I pointed out that all

---

FP friends in the north of Scotland on an almost annual basis. J.P. Neven, 'Ds. Wouter Leendert Tukker', *Terdege*, 10th October 2001.

[176] John Mackenzie, Kishorn (1893–1986) was a missionary. Alex's widow married him in later life. 'Synod Tribute to John Mackenzie, Kishorn, Elder and Missionary', *FPM* Vol. 91 (July 1986): p. 208.

[177] 'But my servant Caleb, because he had another spirit with him, and hath followed me fully, him will I bring into the land whereinto he went; and his seed shall possess it.'

gospel hearers are in one or the other of these classes—and that our believing or not believing determines our fate for eternity.

Thursday 22nd September

Twenty-one attended the prayer meeting. Archie Robertson[178] of Tain took it, from Galatians 6:3–4. 'For if a man think himself to be something, when he is nothing, he deceiveth himself.' He said that no one can say what sin he might fall into, if favourable conditions offered.

Wednesday 12th October

My wife, John and I were in Fearn, where I conducted the service for the Day of Humiliation and Prayer. Mark 1:15 was the text, particularly, 'Repent ye, and believe the gospel.' I said the best contribution we could make towards this day of prayer was to obey this divine command of Christ.

Thursday 13th October

Beauly. Day of Prayer service. Rev. D.A. Macfarlane took as his text Mark 12:34. 'Thou art not far from the kingdom of God.' He said that the man's motive was not clear, that it might have been to get enlightenment, rather than to ensnare him.

Sabbath 16th October

Strathy. In the morning I took 2 Peter 1:10. 'Give diligence to make your calling and election sure.' The points I made were: assurance of salvation is attainable and desirable; diligence is required in the matter; the calling is effectual, from darkness to light, from sin to holiness, from a state of nature to

---

[178] Archibald Robertson (1890–1971) was a North Uist man who served as a missionary from April 1931. 'Archibald Robertson, Missionary, Tain', *FPM* Vol. 77 (February 1972): p. 57.

a state of grace; election springs from the everlasting love of God, is not dependent on anything within us, is the procuring cause of our salvation and all the graces which accompany it.

At 6pm I took 1 Peter 2:21 about following in Christ's footsteps.[179] I mentioned some of his steps. He aimed at the glory of God. He despised the riches and honours of this world. He was a man of prayer and rose before daybreak to pray. He went into the synagogue on the Sabbath day. He had compassion. He set a high value on time.

Tuesday 18th October

Strathy. I was visiting in four houses this afternoon. In the first I read Psalm 130 with a little comment. In another house I read Psalm 51 and part of John 6. Afterwards I went to explore the coastline. What a rugged, inhospitable coast, rocks rising out of the sea to 100 feet in places! I was at Dolly Mackay's[180] for dinner.

Wednesday 19th October

Farr (Bettyhill). I kept the meeting at Farr tonight. I took part of Psalm 89:15 about 'the joyful sound'. The points I made were:

---

[179] 'For even hereunto were ye called: because Christ also suffered for us, leaving us an example, that ye should follow his steps.'

[180] Dolina (née Mackay) was married to Angus Mackay. Her sister, Annie MacAskill, would normally provide a meal to the person conducting the Strathy services but Dolina and Angus also did so occasionally. The Mackays' home was a centre of hospitality in the congregation. Dolina suffered from diabetes and died (in her early sixties) while on a visit to Thurso in 1966. 'Dolly' is the Highland affectionate version of both Dolina and Donald. Another sister, Jessie Robertson Mackay of Strathy Point, Sutherland, was married to the Rev. Malcolm Gillies, Stornoway (1885–1945), with the wedding taking place in Winnipeg, Canada, in 1917.

1. This joyful sound is the good news in the gospel.

2. A description of those to whom the gospel is a joyful sound. They found themselves to be slaves to Satan, oppressed with poverty. They see that through Christ they may be again reinstated in the love and favour of a triune God.

Thursday 20th October

I left Farr early this morning, where I had been staying overnight in Jean Munro's house. I liked my visit to Farr very well. I took the Strathy prayer meeting, fifteen attended. I spoke of the wise and foolish builders in Matthew 7. I made building on sand to mean trusting to anything of the creature—frames, feelings, privileges or profession. I made building on the rock to mean trusting entirely to Christ, his blood, his righteousness and intercession. This will stand for ever.

Sabbath 23rd October

Strathy. In the morning I took the Gentile centurion who came to Christ for his sick servant. Points made: the centurion's humanity, his humility, his faith in Christ's willingness to save. At 6pm I took Matthew 16:24–26[181] on the conditions of discipleship.

---

[181] 'Then said Jesus unto his disciples, If any man will come after me, let him deny himself, and take up his cross, and follow me. For whosoever will save his life shall lose it: and whosoever will lose his life for my sake shall find it. For what is a man profited, if he shall gain the whole world, and lose his own soul? or what shall a man give in exchange for his soul?'

Tuesday 25th October

Strathy. We had the prayer meeting tonight at 7.30, attended by nine. I took Acts 20:27. 'For I have not shunned to declare unto you all the counsel of God.'

Wednesday 26th October

I left Strathy today at 9am on the mail bus.[182] I had a half-hour service at Achvarasdal Care Home.[183] I took Revelation 22:14 with some comment on the words 'Blessed are they that do his commandments'.

I arrived in Wick at 5pm. Rev. MacDonald preached from Psalm 34:8. 'O taste and see that the Lord is good.' He said that the people of God tasted something at the outset of their course which they would like to have again.[184]

Friday 28th October

Wick communion. Question given out by James Davidson was Ephesians 2:13. 'But now in Christ Jesus ye who sometimes were far off are made nigh by the blood of Christ.' I referred to the decided list [wind-induced slant] on the trees of Caithness.

---

[182] These were bus services which combined mail collection with carrying a few passengers, often in remote areas of the UK. The last one in the Highlands ended service in 2017.

[183] This is situated on the outskirts of the village of Reay, Caithness. It closed in June 2018.

[184] The minister for Strathy was Rev. R.R. Sinclair. This is an example of a minister assisting at a communion season also taking the mid-week prayer meeting immediately preceding it.

Saturday 29th October

Wick. I took the 5pm prayer meeting. I took Psalm 22, giving out the line,[185] and read Mark 15. Those who prayed were Robert Watt, Davidson[186] and John Kelly.[187]

Wednesday 2nd November

We kept the fast day for Kilmorack parish today. I went to Dingwall at 7pm to take the service for Mr Macfarlane. I took 1 John 1:6[188] on fellowship with God. I made fellowship to consist in speaking to God, making known our desires, acknowledging our dependence on him for all blessings in providence and grace, going to him as a child to its father believing that that he is able and willing to bestow on us all that

---

[185] This was an English-speaking congregation. The line was often given out in English in Sabbath and week-day services in some Free Presbyterian Church congregations until the late 1960s. In many places it continues in use for English-language psalms on the Sabbath communion service as communicants approach and leave the Lord's Table.

[186] Alex did not specify which of the Davidson brothers (see footnote 151) engaged in prayer.

[187] John S. Kelly was born in Glasgow on the 30th Ocotober 1882. He had professed faith at the Dingwall communion in February 1959. He died in November 1968. His father was a famous Glasgow elder, Donald Kelly (1849–1920) who belonged to Mugary, Portree. His mother was Annie (née Maclean), daughter of Hector Maclean of Hamera in Glendale, Skye. John's sister Mary was the mother of Rev. Alexander Murray, Lairg. For Donald Kelly see 'The late Mr Donald Kelly, Elder, St Jude's, Glasgow', FPM Vol. 24 (April 1920): pp. 372–375. For Hector Maclean, see Roderick MacCowan, The Men of Skye (Edinburgh, Glasgow, Portree: J. Macneilage, 1902; reprinted Edinburgh: Scottish Reformation Society, 2013), pp. 100–112.

[188] 'If we say that we have fellowship with him, and walk in darkness, we lie, and do not the truth.'

is for our good in time and eternity—all this in faith in the sacrifice and intercession of our Lord and Saviour.

Thursday 17th November

Harvest Thanksgiving. Rev. Macfarlane took 1 Kings 18:24. 'And call ye on the name of your gods.' Elijah knew in advance the Lord would answer him by fire. The text may not be thought a relevant text for today, but we should consider that there is no real blessing apart from the sacrifice of Calvary. We have no real right to a teaspoonful of water. People have the 'foot-and-mouth' disease of self-importance, a disease in their walk and in their talk.

In Fearn, I took Genesis 8:20–22. I visited Hugh Mackay,[189] who prayed in Gaelic: 'Oh that thou wouldst give us thy blessing, that we would get knowledge of the unsearchable riches of Christ. For ear hath not heard, neither have entered into the heart of man, the things which God hath prepared for them that love him.' ('O gun tugadh tu dhuinn do bheannachadh, gum faigheadh sinn aithne air saoibhreas do-rannsaichte Chrìosd. Cha chuala cluas, agus cha tàinig ann an cridhe duine, na nithean a dh'ullaich Dia dhaibh-san aig a bheil gràdh dha.' 1 Corinthians 2:9).

Sabbath 18th December

Beauly 12 noon. I took Matthew 8:1–3. The healing of the leper. The points were:

    1. He felt his disease.

    2. His disease was incurable.

    3. He firmly believed that Christ was able to save him.

---

[189] Mr Mackay was the grandfather of Mrs Carine Mackenzie (Inverness) and Rev. Prof. John L. Mackay of the Free Church of Scotland.

I observed that anyone who believes that Christ can save them from their sins and earnestly desires it has saving faith. Christ was expressing his willingness to save all who apply to him as the leper did.

1966

Sabbath 9th January

Shieldaig. This morning I took John 17:3.[190] I stressed that the life we have is ebbing away. We need the endless life. I then dealt with the twofold aspect of God mentioned in the verse—to know him in the law and the gospel.

Monday 10th January

We had the prayer meeting at 7pm. I took Revelation 20:12. 'And the books were opened.' I mentioned some of the books—the Bible, conscience, memory, the creatures, and the Book of Life.

Sabbath 16th January

Beauly 6pm. I was led at last to Matthew 11:2–6. John the Baptist sent to Jesus to ask if he was the Messiah. I gave as my view that it was through a fit of unbelief that he did so. It seems the more obvious sense, I think.

---

[190] 'And this is life eternal, that they might know thee the only true God, and Jesus Christ, whom thou hast sent.'

Monday 17th January

I was in Dingwall this afternoon and visited three houses after doing some business. Much visiting is no easy task but I believe it is a reliable asset for a minister or elder to be a good visitor. The people love it and will remember very well when your last visit was.

Saturday 22nd January

We heard with grief of heart of William Logan's death after his plane crashed into Craig Dunain en route from Edinburgh to Dalcross. I was greatly impressed at the tragedy, a man who since the New Year was sitting at my fireside. It is a loud voice to the land because he was a man who refrained from working on Sabbath.

Sabbath 23rd January

Beauly, noon. I referred at the close of the service to the untimely death of William Logan as a token of God's holy displeasure. By refraining from Sabbath work, he brought the matter of the Sabbath into prominence in a godless and materialistic age, thus setting an example to employers of labour all over Scotland.[191]

Thursday 27th January

Inverness communion. Rev. Malcom MacSween (Oban) preached at 11am from the words 'Mercy rejoiceth against judgment' in James 2:13. Points:

    1. How is it that God's mercy rejoices against judgment?

    2. Why is it that mercy rejoices against judgment?

    3. When does this take place?

---

[191] Alex saw the loss of an influential Christian such as Mr Logan as a sign of God's displeasure.

Friday 28th January

Inverness communion. The Question was given out by Robert Watt: 'He that hath the son hath life.' About twelve were called to speak and another dozen were on the list but not called. We got out a little after 10pm.

Sabbath 30th January

Inverness communion, Action Sermon. In the church Mr MacSween took Hebrews 1:3. 'Who being the brightness of his glory, and the express image of his person.' Points:
  1. What he is.
  2. What he has done.
  3. What he enjoys as a result of his work.

Thursday 24th February

Prayer meeting, about twenty attended. I took John 15:5, particularly, 'I am the vine, ye are the branches'. The vine is a most fruitful tree. It is useless if not supported. If barren, it is useless for any other purpose. It needs pruning in order to fruitfulness. A caution: beware of being cumberers of the ground.

Wednesday 2nd March

Ullapool communion. Rev. Alfred MacDonald[192] took the meeting at 7pm on Colossians 1:29. 'Whereunto I also labour, striving according to his working, which worketh in me mightily.' He said that we have reason to fear that we are not striving as we should after holiness but indulging in sloth. I

---

[192] Oban-born Mr MacDonald is a brother of the late Rev. Fraser MacDonald, Portree. He served as minister in Ingwenya, Zimbabwe, from 1959 until 1965 and has been minister of the Gairloch congregation since November 1965. He tutored divinity students from 1986 to 1995 and from 2000 to 2002.

visited Rev. D.N. Macleod who is on his bed and over 90 years old, but his faculties are quite good.[193] He asked me to pray.

Thursday 3rd March

Ullapool. Rev. Alfred MacDonald took the morning service as Rev. Fraser MacDonald had yet to arrive because the Loch Seaforth went ashore on the rocks at Kyle.[194] He took James 4:10.[195] Rev. Fraser MacDonald arrived in time for the 6pm service and took Romans 13:11. 'And that, knowing the time, that now it is high time to awake out of sleep: for now is our salvation nearer than when we believed.' He said there were three conditions favourable to sleep: darkness, quietness and comfort.

Friday 4th March

The Question was given out by A. Macleod[196] and was 1 Corinthians 6:20.[197] Opening the Question, Rev. Alfred

---

[193] Donald Norman Macleod (1872–1967) was a North Uist man who pastored the Harris Free Presbyterian congregation from 1911 until accepting a call from Ullapool in 1924, where he laboured until his death. His 'plainness and directness' in preaching won him the attention of his listeners. A series of biographical sketches by Rev. John Macleod ran in the FPM from August to December 1974.

[194] A mailboat which linked Stornoway (Isle of Lewis) with the mainland ports of Mallaig and Kyle of Lochalsh from 1947 until 1972. Seventeen years later, the boat ran aground on Cleit Rock in the Sound of Gunna (between Tiree and Coll) on 22nd March 1973 and was subsequently scrapped.

[195] 'Humble yourselves in the sight of the Lord, and he shall lift you up.'

[196] Angus Macleod (1899–1975) and his wife Marjory (née Nicolson, died 1988) were well-respected figures in the community. He was the father of the Rev. K.D. Macleod, formerly the minister of South

MacDonald said, 'The eyes of believers are opened to see something of the price paid for them.'

Monday 14th March

After a doctor's appointment I visited Mr Macfarlane in the manse. I never saw a man so careful in conversation not to infringe on the laws of charity toward all men; not, however, a false charity as is too common in our day but speaking the truth in love.

Sabbath 20th March

John took the evening service in Beauly on Matthew 6 about seeking first the kingdom of God. He observed that no one in a natural state will seek the kingdom of God. He dwelt a lot on the work of the law, then offered a full-orbed gospel. I was quite pleased with all he said—sound doctrine and words of truth and soberness from beginning to end.

Wednesday 23rd March

I am afraid that in our day men are more eager to hear what the radio and television has to say, if it happens to clash with the family worship, when the singing of God's praise was wont to resound from our Highland homes. Satan has now taken the field and demands attention. Very few can resist him. There is a party within the heart that listens to him.

Harris, presently minister of Inverness since 2017. 'Angus Macleod, Elder, Ullapool', *FPM* Vol. 81 (July 1976): pp. 251–253.

[197] 'For ye are bought with a price: therefore glorify God in your body, and in your spirit, which are God's.'

Friday 1st April

I felt it was the Lord's will for me to go with my wife to visit three old ladies in Resolis. They got a great uplift by our visit. I felt I had good guidance in going.

Sabbath 3rd April

I took Acts 9 and spoke of the leading features in Paul's conversion:

    1. He saw light from heaven.

    2. He inquired what God wished him to do.

    3. He began to pray.

    4. He separated from his old companions.

Saturday 2nd July

Beauly communion. I don't remember when I got a more pleasant surprise: two new members. I was continually praying for it but I did not know what quarter they were to come from. It was a tonic to my soul. Praise the Lord.

Sabbath 3rd July

Beauly. Rev. Alexander MacAskill took the Action Sermon on Song of Solomon 2:1–3. I was impressed with the manner in which he described the Person of Christ, God and man in two distinct natures. We were never so hard pressed to find room in the church.

At 6.30 we were so crammed I had to sit in the pulpit. Rev. Alfred MacDonald took Matthew 11:28. 'Come unto me.' He left such as refused without excuse.

Monday 4th July

In the Gaelic thanksgiving service, Mr MacAskill took Psalm 84:5. 'Blessed is the man whose strength is in thee.' Rev. Alfred MacDonald took Romans 16:20. 'And the God of peace shall bruise Satan under your feet shortly.' He spoke a lot about Satan and how he seeks to break the peace in families and congregations and in the church, and our need to be strong in the Lord.

Friday 8th July

Tain communion. The Question was given by Archie Robertson. Isaiah 12:1.[198] He wanted marks of those mentioned in the verse to distinguish them from those who are strangers to this experience. I did not feel liberty to speak much. It is one thing to speak about God's anger but to feel a flash of it in one's conscience is another matter, and one which I pray God I may never experience. I desire to praise him for showing me the way of salvation and making Christ precious to me, in a milder manner than he has done to many others.

Tuesday 19th July

While crossing a high dyke today I fell headlong backwards, with a violent jolt when my right shoulder hit the ground. So I am a bruised and battered man and can hardly do anything for myself. However, my sins are the cause of it. I am sure God is right in all he doeth.

Friday 5th August

Dingwall communion. I gave out the Question in Lamentations 3:25.[199] Fourteen were called to speak and many more could have been.

---

[198] 'And in that day thou shalt say, O Lord, I will praise thee: though thou wast angry with me, thine anger is turned away, and thou comfortedst me.'

[199] 'The Lord is good unto them that wait for him, to the soul that seeketh him.'

Sabbath 7th August

Dingwall communion. Rev. MacLean preached from the immutability of the promise and the consolation that flows from it in Hebrews 6:17–18. We had over 120 communicants at the Lord's Supper. The minister remarked that one third of the large congregation were communicants. I suppose that can rarely be said anywhere else. We had a great day of the gospel. Such as fall from this eminence will go deep into perdition. Here I am on Monday mourning over my unprofitableness. The Lord gave me strength to do my duties, exceeding all my expectations.

Friday 19th August

Bonar Bridge communion. Question given out by Alec John Davidson[200] in 1 John 1:7.[201] Archie Robertson said, 'If I were asked "Are you born again?" I would be afraid to reply in the negative.' We had seven or eight to speak.

Saturday 20th August

Raasay. I left Dingwall at 11.20 and then had a comfortable sea journey here from Kyle. I now need preparation for the morrow, for I feel I have 'nothing wherewith to feed the multitude'.

---

[200] Alec John Davidson died in January 1978 after 38 years as an elder in the Halkirk-Helmsdale congregation. He was described as 'faithful and discerning' in the church courts. 'Tribute to the late Mr A.J. Davidson, Elder, Helmsdale', *Synod Proceedings, May 1978* (Glasgow, 1978), pp. 28–29.

[201] 'But if we walk in the light, as he is in the light, we have fellowship one with another, and the blood of Jesus Christ his Son cleanseth us from all sin.'

Sabbath 21st August

Raasay. I took at noon 'Look unto me, and be ye saved, all the ends of the earth' (Isaiah 45:22). Points were:

1. The one speaking.
2. The people addressed—all the ends of the earth.
3. What is promised—salvation.

At 5pm I took Hebrews 10. 'But this man.'

Wednesday 24th August

Raasay. About 80 attended the prayer meeting. I took the publican's prayer 'God be merciful to me a sinner' in Luke 18:13. I spoke a little about the Pharisee, then noticed that the publican prayed to the right person—God in Christ. He prayed for mercy not justice. He prayed as a sinner. Those praying were Ewan,[202] Charlie Macleod[203] and Roddy.[204]

Friday 26th August

Isle of Rona, Raasay. At 10am we went up to the light-house in a Land Rover; this was my first time on wheels on Rona. We had a service in Arnish[205] about 1pm. I took 'Let not your heart be troubled' in John 14:1. There were fifteen present.

---

[202] Ewan Macrae was pier master in Raasay. He was a brother of Tommy Macrae, Glasgow and Dumbarton. 'Ewan Macrae, Raasay', *FPM* Vol. 76 (November 1971): pp. 344–345.

[203] Mr Macleod was a Raasay-born policeman who served for many years in Edinburgh. 'Charles Macleod, Edinburgh', *FPM* Vol. 82 (May 1977): pp. 180–182.

[204] This may have been Roderick Macleod, an elder who died in 1979. 'Tribute to the late Roderick Macleod, Raasay', *Synod Proceedings, May 1980* (Glasgow, 1980), pp. 26–27.

[205] Arnish is a small settlement at the north of Raasay. There is an unrelated place of the same name near Stornoway, Isle of Lewis.

Saturday 27th August

Roddy and I left Arnish about 1.30pm in lovely weather. About halfway, on top of the hill, we sat and sang a few verses.

Sabbath 28th August

Raasay. At noon I preached in Galatians 6:3[206] and at 5pm in Acts 20:27, 'For I have not shunned to declare unto you the whole counsel of God.' A large congregation.

Tuesday 30th August

Raasay. About seventy attended the prayer meeting. I took 'Whosoever drinketh of this water shall thirst again'. John 4:13. I tried to trace the analogy between water and the grace of God, and how the water of life is not valued when it abounds. Water is indispensable, cleanses as nothing else can, seeks to the lowest place, ascends as high as its source if confined, and is restless until it reaches the ocean.

Friday 9th September

I am 77 today. 'Having therefore obtained help of God, I continue unto this day.' (Acts 26:22).

Sabbath 18th September

In Beauly I took the parable of the steward in Luke 16. We waste what we are entrusted with: our time, our money, our influence, the Bible, and the privileges of a gospel ministry. On another day we will be called to account for all of these.

Tuesday 18th October

Robert Watt died at 2am.

---

[206] 'For if a man think himself to be something, when he is nothing, he deceiveth himself.'

Thursday 17th November

Rev. D.A. Macfarlane preached at the Kilmorack Harvest Thanksgiving service on the words 'His name alone is excellent' in Psalm 148:13. He spoke a good deal about the words 'his people's horn' as the symbol of power. He said beasts often gore others with their horns. Christ gored the enemies of his people: death and the grave. He gored Satan in the sense that he cannot hurt God's people.

Thursday 29th December

Kilmorack prayer meeting, twenty attended. I took the words 'And yet there is room' in Luke 14:22. These words imply that there is a limited time, there is room now, another day is coming in which there will be no room. The application is that we must make sure of being in time, the supper is the last meal of the day. If you refuse that then you will go famishing to the long night of eternity.

1967

Thursday 5th January

Prayer meeting, sixteen attended. I took the man who built his house on the rock, from Luke 6. The rock is Jesus Christ. The rock is the emblem of stability and perpetuity; it is the best for a foundation. So is Christ.

Sabbath 8th January

Beauly, 6pm. I took Hebrews 12:1.[207] The Christian is like one running a race. He must discard needless clothing. He must look steadfastly to Jesus. He must have patience and perseverance.

Monday 9th January

I read recently of a man looking at famous pictures in an art gallery, who said he didn't see anything special about them. The custodian, hearing him, said, 'Remember it is not the pictures that are on trial but the visitors.'

---

[207] 'Wherefore seeing we also are compassed about with so great a cloud of witnesses, let us lay aside every weight, and the sin which doth so easily beset us, and let us run with patience the race that is set before us.'

Wednesday 11th January

I attended the funeral of Mrs M. I insisted on our minister making a prayer. What a prayer! The fragrance of Calvary was in every sentence.

Thursday 26th January

Inverness communion. Rev. John Colquhoun preached an able sermon from 'We have piped unto you, and ye have not danced' (Matthew 11:17). He spoke of the marketplace of free grace and the wares sold at it: Christ and all his benefits.

Friday 27th January

The Question was given out by Finlay Beaton in Romans 5:1.[208] There were nineteen on the roll and twelve were called. I liked the Question very well. John Mackenzie, speaking in Gaelic, said, 'If your sins didn't keep an hour's sleep from you, you have reason to fear.'

Saturday 28th January

One new member. Mr Colquhoun preached from Song of Solomon 8:13. 'Thou that dwellest in the gardens, the companions hearken to thy voice: cause me to hear it.' What are the gardens? They are the means of grace, secret prayer, where two or three are gathered. A woman who was alone at a prayer meeting said that the Father, Son and Holy Spirit were there and that they had a glorious time.

---

[208] 'Therefore being justified by faith, we have peace with God through our Lord Jesus Christ.'

Sabbath 29th January

Inverness communion. Action Sermon was in Isaiah 53:5.[209] Four tables.[210]

Thursday 2nd February

Dingwall communion. In the English at 12 noon, Rev. Donald M. Macleod, Stornoway, took Isaiah 59:1–2.[211] He asked, 'Are you persuaded that it is only the Lord that can cure you?'

Friday 3rd February

Dingwall communion. John Kelly asked on the way in if he could give out the Question. He asked for marks of the fruits of repentance as in Ezekiel 33:11.[212] About twelve were called to speak and a further six were left out.

Saturday 4th February

One person was received as a member. He appears to be a truly changed young man. Praise the Lord, his Spirit is still striving with us.

---

[209] 'But he was wounded for our transgressions, he was bruised for our iniquities: the chastisement of our peace was upon him; and with his stripes we are healed.'

[210] Two years later Alex noted 150 communicants at the Lord's Supper in Inverness; four tables would probably have been needed on that occasion too.

[211] 'Behold, the Lord's hand is not shortened, that it cannot save; neither his ear heavy, that it cannot hear: but your iniquities have separated between you and your God, and your sins have hid his face from you, that he will not hear.'

[212] 'Say unto them, As I live, saith the Lord God, I have no pleasure in the death of the wicked; but that the wicked turn from his way and live: turn ye, turn ye from your evil ways; for why will ye die, O house of Israel?'

Monday 6th February

Gaelic—Mr Macleod took Joshua 1:9.[213] He said Joshua needed the Word of God in setting out to lead Israel to Canaan. At 7pm he took Psalm 31. Our love to Christ cannot be too fervent. We may inordinately love the creature. God's people love his Sabbath, Word, ordinances and people.

Thursday 9th February

Beauly prayer meeting. Rev. D.A. Macfarlane took the words 'Out of his belly shall flow rivers of living water' in John 7:38. The allusion may be to the smitten rock in the wilderness—from the belly of this rock flowed living waters. You may say the rock was in the belly of Peter and John. If you have love to the truth you have rivers of living water. You may feel a parched land but if Christ is within you, you have the fulness of eternity. Although you mourn for your shortcomings—how little you love Christ, for example—yet you have a holy love to his commandments.

Thursday 2nd March

Twenty-five attended the prayer meeting. I took John 15 and spoke of God choosing his people to bear fruit. Fruit-bearing consists of growing in grace, sinking in self-loathing, exalting Christ, renouncing all merit in ourselves, ascribing all we are to the free grace of God, desiring Christ to have all the glory, and for him 'to be to us wisdom, righteousness, sanctification and redemption'.

---

[213] 'Have not I commanded thee? Be strong and of a good courage; be not afraid, neither be thou dismayed: for the Lord thy God is with thee whithersoever thou goest.'

Thursday 9th March

Wild weather; attendance was twenty. I endeavoured to make some remarks on the resurrection as the pivot round which the ages revolve, the greatest event of all time, the key-stone in the arch of salvation, and the foundation of Christianity. It proves that Christ has paid our debts, proved his divinity and humanity, that there is no condemnation now for the believer, and that they will all rise again at the latter day.

Sabbath 16th March

Beauly 6pm. I took the promise to give them 'Canaan's land' in Psalm 105:11. I mentioned some points of similarity between the land of Canaan and heaven. Canaan was the land of promise. They found everything ready: houses, wells and vineyards. They entered after a long wilderness journey. They had to cross the Jordan. It was not Moses who took them in but Joshua. Jesus is our leader to the heavenly Canaan.

Thursday 11th May

About twenty-five attended the prayer meeting. I took the 'strangers and pilgrims' in Hebrews 11:13. It means they were not at home in this world. They love to talk of heaven. They have spiritual minds. They are born from above. They are always seeking marks of being on the right road. They believe there is 'no continuing city' here. They daily seek preparation for going home.

Wednesday 7th June

Shieldaig communion begins tomorrow. At the prayer meeting Rev. Alex MacAskill took Psalm 91:1. 'He that dwelleth in the secret place.' Few know of this secret place. It is God alone that can show it. Love of God is a secret matter. It is one thing to speak of it, another matter to experience it.

Nothing will satisfy a living soul but that which will last for ever.

Friday 30th June

Beauly communion. Question (at 6.30pm) was Matthew 16:16. 'Thou art the Christ, the son of the living God.' It was opened by Rev. Lachlan Macleod,[214] who said that Peter grasped the essential doctrine that Jesus is the Son of God. About ten spoke, we were out about 9pm. Closed by Mr Morrison, Uist, who said, 'We heard many precious things tonight.'

Friday 21st July

I attended J's funeral. Finlay prayed to begin with, John Tallach led the singing, giving out the line. I then read the last part of 1 Corinthians 15. I prayed at the end and Rev. William Grant gave the exhortation at the Mitchell Hill cemetery. So J, like Mr Fearing, crossed over.[215]

Friday 11th August

Alex Beaton, Struan,[216] told me the Scripture was much in his mind: 'Thou, with thy counsel, while I live, / wilt me conduct and guide.'[217]

---

[214] Rev. Lachlan Macleod (1918–1998) was a well-loved Skye-born preacher. By this time he was minister in Greenock having served in Uig, Lewis, from 1953 until 1965. 'The Rev. Lachlan Macleod', *FPM* Vol. 105 (May 2000): pp. 139–145.

[215] Mr Fearing was a character in John Bunyan's *Pilgrim's Progress* for whom the Lord restrained his enemies as he passed over the valley of the shadow of death.

[216] Alexander Beaton (1892–1980) served as missionary in Struan from around 1935 until 1972. 'The Late Alexander Beaton, Totardor, Struan, Skye', *FPM* Vol. 86 (August 1981): pp. 266–267.

[217] Psalm 73:24, metrical version.

Saturday 12th August

Left Portree for Applecross. I left Kyle about 3.15pm, arriving at Toscaig pier[218] about 4.30.

Sabbath 13th August

Applecross. At 6pm I took Luke 1:79.[219] I spoke a little about this title of Christ's, 'the dayspring'. Those on whom the dayspring is arisen see where they are, see the way to go, and begin to work. The prospect before them is the eternal day.

Wednesday 16th August

Applecross prayer meeting; about thirty attended. I took Luke 6:47–48, the man who built his house on the rock. Man is represented as a builder for eternity. The one in the text is a wise builder, using the line and plummet of God's Word. The foundation he builds on is the solid rock Christ. He gets the stone from the quarry of Scripture. This building stands un-moved when the tempest beats upon it.

Friday 18th August

I attended the funeral of John Grant,[220] Inverness. I then got a lift from Inverness to Bonar Bridge where the Question

---

[218] Toscaig is the most southerly of the small settlements that extend south from Applecross village on the west coast of the Applecross peninsula. The village was the terminus for a motor boat service which linked the peninsula with Kyle of Lochalsh from the 1950s to the 1970s.

[219] 'To give light to them that sit in darkness and in the shadow of death, to guide our feet into the way of peace.'

[220] John Grant (c.1881–1967) was a brother of the Rev. William Grant. He was married to Bella Grant (see footnote for 30th April 1957). Mr Grant was a banker and from 1924 to 1960 he was General Treasurer of the Free Presbyterian Church. Converted while

127

was given out by D. Maclennan[221] in John 10:27. 'My sheep hear my voice.'

Tuesday 22ⁿᵈ August

Induction at Daviot. Rev. D.A. Macfarlane took the service from Hebrews 13:10.[222] He said: 'We can only wade on the fringes of this ocean. There is a mine here of diamonds and riches with which to fill the pockets of your soul.'

Wednesday 4th October

Gairloch communion. Went to the prayer meeting in Opinan[223] at 7pm. Rev. D.M. Macleod took Psalm 25:6.[224] He said that no one can say the Bible is the infallible Word of God but by the teaching of heaven.

Friday 6th October

Sandy Maclean[225] gave out the Question in 1 Peter 2:10.[226] He asked for marks of those that 'are now the people of God'. About seven spoke.

---

working in Haddington, he knew the Rev. Neil Cameron (Glasgow) and the Rev. Donald Macfarlane (Raasay and Dingwall) in his youth. He was an elder in the Inverness congregation. 'Obituary: John Grant, Inverness', *FPM* Vol. 76 (October 1971): pp. 309–312.

[221] Donald Maclennan (1929–1988), was a respected Sutherland man of Harris descent. He was a missionary in the Dornoch-Rogart congregation. 'Mr Donald Maclennan, Missionary, Dornoch and Rogart', *FPM* Vol. 95 (May 1990): pp. 152–154.

[222] 'We have an altar, whereof they have no right to eat which serve the tabernacle.'

[223] A township around 9 miles (14 km) south of Gairloch.

[224] 'Remember, O Lord, thy tender mercies and thy lovingkindnesses; for they have been ever of old.'

[225] Sandy Maclean (1893–1975) was made an elder in the Gairloch congregation in 1946 and served as a missionary in the Laide section of the congregation for over thirty years before it was made a sepa-

Thursday 12th October

Beauly 12 noon. Day of Prayer. Rev. D.A. Macfarlane took Romans 8:6. 'To be carnally minded is death.' He gave as examples of carnal-mindedness: Cain, the scribes and Pharisees, Paul in his unregenerate days. He also gave examples of the spiritually minded: if you are in heart harmony with the 51st Psalm; if you love Psalm 119:133: 'O let my footsteps in thy word / aright still ordered be.'

Saturday 28th October

We don't see the same preparation for the Sabbath now. I remember in my childhood days hearing a man of the world saying to his daughter-in-law, 'It's time for you to stop knitting when it's 8pm on a Saturday night.'

Thursday 9th November

Dingwall, Harvest Thanksgiving. Mr Macfarlane took 'Give us this day our daily bread' in Matthew 6:11. He spoke much about the procuring cause and fountain of all our blessing.

Donald Kelly[227] was in Beauly at 7pm. When I asked what he preached from he said, 'I got a minister from Helmsdale to

---

rate pastoral charge. 'Alexander Maclean, Gairloch', *FPM* Vol. 81 (June 1976): pp. 216–218.

[226] 'Which in time past were not a people, but are now the people of God: which had not obtained mercy, but now have obtained mercy.'

[227] Donald Shaw Kelly was brought up in Aultnagar near Lairg, Sutherland. A nephew of John Kelly in the Beauly congregation, Donald served as an elder, clerk to the Kirk Session, church officer and precentor in the Dingwall congregation. He was manager of the DE Shoe shop in the town. He died on 26th April 1997, aged 78.

preach for me.' Afterwards I discovered that he read from a book of sermons.[228]

Sabbath 19th November

Beauly 6pm. James Tallach[229] took Ruth 2:12.[230] His points were:

    1. How did she come to trust?

    2. What it is to trust 'under the wings' of the God of Israel.

    3. The consequences of trusting him.

He said that Boaz told the reapers to let handfuls fall for Ruth to lift, and that the New Testament Boaz [Christ] will order his messengers to speak comfort to needy souls.

Thursday 7th December

Beauly prayer meeting, fifteen attended. I took 1 Corinthians 16:22.[231] I gave marks of such as love Christ. They seek communion with him. They think highly of him.

---

[228] The book would have been John Mackay, *Memoir of the Late Rev. John Macdonald, A.M., Minister of the Free Church at Helmsdale,* (Edinburgh: Johnstone and Hunter, 1856). John Mac-Donald (1800–1854) became a preacher in Helmsdale in 1837 but was not ordained there until after the Disruption in July 1843.

[229] James Ross Tallach is a son of the Stornoway manse who served as a medical missionary for many years in Rhodesia (renamed as the Republic of Zimbabwe following independence in 1980). Following divinity training, he was ordained in 1980 and continued to work in Zimbabwe. He pastored Raasay from 1983 until 2009, when he became minister of Stornoway, where he still serves.

[230] 'The Lord recompense thy work, and a full reward be given thee of the Lord God of Israel, under whose wings thou art come to trust.'

[231] 'If any man love not the Lord Jesus Christ, let him be Anathema Maranatha.'

They love to attend where the gospel is preached. They lay themselves out to serve him.

Sabbath 17th December

Beauly. At 6pm John took Hebrews 9:27. 'And as it is appointed unto men once to die, but after this the judgment.' All that he had was pure gospel.

Thursday 28th December

I took the unfaithful steward in Luke 16 and the provision he made in view of being deprived of his post:

1. We are all stewards in the sense that we, our goods and time belong to God; we are responsible for using the same to the glory of God.

2. We have received our notice that the stewardship is going to an end. Death is coming to deprive us of it.

3. We must give account for the way we have used the privileges entrusted to us.

4. The unjust steward came to a point at which he 'was resolved what to do'. So it is with the awakened sinner. He finds himself lost. He gets anxious and alarmed. He begins to seek preparation for what lies ahead.

1968

Monday 1st January

For the New Year's Day service I took John 14:6. 'Jesus saith unto him, I am the way, the truth, and the life.' How do I know if I am on the way spoken of in the text? When one travels from one place to another, looking back he sees the place he left becoming smaller and smaller, and the place he is going looks larger. On the heavenly course, the world—its sports and pastimes, pleasure and company—is empty and as nothing, while on the other hand, God, Christ, heaven, death and judgment seem the all-important things.

Sabbath 7th January

Dingwall, noon. I again took John 14:6. I stressed the fact that the old way by the covenant of works is now blocked by the landslide of Adam's fall so the way to heaven by the old route is now closed to mankind. We must now go by the new and living way provided by the incarnation and death of our Lord and Saviour Jesus Christ.

Tuesday 9th January

I am reading at night in John 3 from which we can gather valuable lessons. Nicodemus came by night, whatever for? It was good that he came. We may also be coming by night in the sense that we try to conceal what the Lord hath done for us, when we are ashamed to be seen praying or reading the Bible, or when we don't profess publicly what the Lord did for us. For myself I got over that long ago and feel like the Psalmist: 'Then shall I not be sham'd, when I / thy precepts all respect.'[232]

Friday 12th January

The area has been in the severe grip of winter since the 1st of January My wife and I went to an out-of-the-way place in the Heights of Kiltarlity where an old couple were short of provisions as no van was calling on them. They were delighted to see her, it is such an isolated place.

Thursday 25th January

Inverness communion. Mr MacAskill, Lochinver, took Lamentations 5:21. 'Turn thou us unto thee, O Lord, and we shall be turned; renew our days as of old.' His points were:

1. The request before us: 'Turn thou us.'

2. The confidence God's people have in the midst of their troubles.

3. The grounds on which they made the request. We think it is in verse 19, 'Thou, O Lord, remainest for ever.'

He told of a woman who had a croft and no one to work it. She was up early looking for someone to do the work. The cause of her being stirred up over it was her helplessness. No

---

[232] Psalm 119:6, metrical version.

matter how low God's people come, they have confidence that Christ is able to save them.

Friday 26th January

The Question was given out by John Gunn.[233] Acts 15:11.[234] A. Maclean, Strath,[235] said, 'This people can recall a day in which they had no desire for grace.' Ten were called to speak; the service lasted three hours.

Sabbath 28th January

Action Sermon. Hebrews 4:14–16. Mr MacAskill's points were:

    1. Those addressed.

    2. The twofold statement made.

    3. The exhortation to come boldly to the throne of grace. He said, 'God's people will never forget what he has done for them.'

Monday 29th January

1 Samuel 22:23.[236] Mr MacAskill. He said we should notice what David said to Abiathar. Christ can make death sweet to you, although you fear it now.

---

[233] Mr Gunn was born in Skerray (Sutherland-shire). He was a hearer of Rev. Neil Cameron while working as a policeman in Glasgow, and later an elder in Inverness where he died in 1981. 'John Gunn, Inverness', *FPM* Vol. 86 (October 1981): pp. 328–330.

[234] 'But we believe that through the grace of the Lord Jesus Christ we shall be saved, even as they.'

[235] This was almost certainly Sandy Maclean, Gairloch. See footnote for Friday 6th October 1967.

[236] 'Abide thou with me, fear not: for he that seeketh my life seeketh thy life: but with me thou shalt be in safeguard.'

Thursday 1st February

Dingwall communion. At 11am Rev. Donald Nicolson, North Tolsta,[237] took Matthew 5:4.[238] He said mourning follows sin. Sin promises happiness but cannot fulfil it. The people of God mourn and rejoice at the same time.

Friday 2nd February

I gave out the Question in John 6:54.[239] In opening it, Mr Nicolson said, 'Christ took a body of flesh and blood in order to die, satisfy the law and destroy death.'

Monday 12th February

After hospital visiting, my wife and I went to the Inverness prayer meeting. Finlay Beaton took it and spoke on Psalm 60, a very difficult portion. At first he spoke a great deal about the patriarchs and the promises about the Messiah. But when he came to the gospel it was like a breath of the air of heaven—the necessity of the atonement, and the fruits of it.

Thursday 15th February

Beauly prayer meeting; eighteen attended. I took Hebrews 2:3. 'How shall we escape, if we neglect so great salvation?' A great salvation has been provided at great cost, for a great number, from so great a death, for great sinners by the great God who made heaven and earth. We are in great danger if

---

[237] Donald Nicolson (1911–2001) was assistant to Rev. Kenneth Macrae, Stornoway Free Church, before becoming an FP minister in 1967. He held pastorates in North Tolsta (Isle of Lewis), Raasay and Glendale (Isle of Skye). 'Obituary: Rev Donald Nicolson', *FPM* Vol. 107 (March 2002): pp. 84–87.

[238] 'Blessed are they that mourn: for they shall be comforted.'

[239] 'Whoso eateth my flesh, and drinketh my blood, hath eternal life; and I will raise him up at the last day.'

we neglect it, we shut the way of escape from sin, Satan, death and hell.

Tuesday 20th February

I was reading this morning about the dry bones in Ezekiel 37. There is great encouragement for poor sinners as we hear of life coming into dry bones. Such we are in our natural state, without breath or motion any more than these dry bones. God's people desire and pray for a breeze of the Holy Spirit to blow upon them.

Wednesday 28th February

Ullapool communion. The Stratherrick minister [Rev. A. McPherson] took John 14:26,[240] speaking of the Comforter. Love is the principal grace. Where there is love to Christ there is love to the Word. It should shame us how unmoved we are when we read of Christ's sufferings. I was in Hector Campbell's for supper.[241]

Friday 1st March

Ullapool. The Question was given out by Hector Campbell in Matthew 28:5.[242]

---

[240] 'But the Comforter, which is the Holy Ghost, whom the Father will send in my name, he shall teach you all things, and bring all things to your remembrance, whatsoever I have said unto you.'

[241] Hector Campbell (1897–1975) was recalled as a spiritually-minded man given to secret prayer and was noted for hospitality. He lived first on the Scoraig peninsula and then on Pulteney Street, Ullapool. 'Hector Campbell, Scoraig and Ullapool', FPM Vol. 81 (February 1976): pp. 54–56.

[242] 'And the angel answered and said unto the women, Fear not ye: for I know that ye seek Jesus, which was crucified.'

Monday 18th March

Inverness prayer meeting. Neil Ross[243] took it from the verse in Deuteronomy 33:29. 'Happy art thou, O Israel.' I think it was his first time in Inverness.

Sabbath 24th March

Beauly 6pm. I took the parable of the fig tree in Luke 13. The outstanding lesson is that we must bear fruit or be cut down. Fruit-bearing consists in love, peace, resignation to the will of God, and looking to Christ for all we need.

Thursday 28th March

Twenty-three attended Beauly prayer meeting. I took 1 John 1:9.[244] I mentioned four steps the believer goes through in connection with his sins.

1. He comes to see them in the light of God's law which is exceeding broad, holy and spiritual.

2. He confesses his sins to God. By so doing he honours all the attributes of the deity.

3. He forsakes them. 'What have I to do any more with idols?'

4. The most difficult step—he hates sin as the Psalmist: 'I therefore ev'ry way that's false / with all my heart do hate.'[245]

---

[243] Neil M. Ross was born in Ferintosh in 1935. He was inducted as minister of Ullapool in November 1978, where he was pastor until accepting a call from Dingwall in 1992. He retired in 2017. Mr Ross edited *The Young People's Magazine* from 1984 until 1994 and then the *Free Presbyterian Magazine* from 1995 until 2000.

[244] 'If we confess our sins, he is faithful and just to forgive us our sins, and to cleanse us from all unrighteousness.'

[245] Psalm 119:104, metrical version.

Monday 1st April

I twisted my ankle which caused me to yell with pain. However, I bow to God's will. 'All things work together for good.' His ways are past finding out. Accidents may visit God's people, even when they daily look to him for safety. 'What I do thou knowest not now; but thou shalt know hereafter' (John 13:7).

Saturday 6th April

Rev. D.N. MacLeod (Ullapool) said, 'One thing common to all the Lord's people is the hiding of his countenance.' I find it so.

Sabbath 21st April

At Beauly at 6pm. I took Luke 15:21.[246] The parable of the prodigal son shows God's readiness to pardon whenever the sinner is ready to value it.

Tuesday 23rd April

I have to admit reluctantly that I am 'going back' [less able than previously] and unfit for much manual labour. It is strange, we seem to be ashamed of growing old and losing our strength and being unable to do any work. Of course, sin is the cause of it, which is a shame to men. However, if it would teach us to seek the life which is found in Christ, a life which will never age or grow weary. Who can understand the glory of the spiritual body with which believers are to be raised at the resurrection?

---

[246] 'And the son said unto him, Father, I have sinned against heaven, and in thy sight, and am no more worthy to be called thy son.'

Thursday 25th April

At the prayer meeting I took a passage which I'd been reading last night at worship, 1 Corinthians 13:13.[247] Praise the Lord—I got fair liberty and the attention of the people which is something to be thankful for. I just wonder how I get through at all, oppressed as I am with poverty, Psalm 113.

Wednesday 1st May

Inverness. Finlay Beaton persuaded me to take the Gaelic prayer meeting. I was led to Simon the Pharisee and the woman who was a sinner who washed Christ's feet, in Luke 7. Those praying were Finlay Beaton, Kenny 'The Home',[248] and John Gunn.

Thursday 9th May

At Beauly prayer meeting, twenty-eight people attended. I took 2 Corinthians 5:17. 'Therefore if any man be in Christ, he is a new creature.' To be in Christ means to be in a refuge. Some of the things that are new and inseparable from the new creature are: he has new ends in what he does, he has new company, he speaks the language of Canaan, and he looks on God's creation with new eyes. As he looks on the heavens, he sees in them unmistakeable signs of his tremendous power and Godhead.

---

[247] 'And now abideth faith, hope, charity, these three; but the greatest of these is charity.'

[248] This is thought to be Kenny MacAskill who, with his Applecross-born wife Flora, had lived in Glasgow where he worked in the police force. They retired to his native village of Bracadale on the Isle of Skye, where he was an elder. In old age, after Flora's death, he eventually moved to the Church's Home of Rest at Ballifeary House, Inverness.

Saturday 18th May

Here am I, afraid as usual in view of Sabbath duties and not feeling equal to it. I feel hard, God silent, and the Bible a sealed book. I know that without the Holy Spirit I am only as a 'tinkling cymbal'. All I can do is to pray about it. I can no more command the Spirit than bring rain from heaven. I cannot even settle on a passage, but I have to take some subject when the time comes. I wonder if any of my fellow men who speak in God's name feel as I do. I just feel as one turned upside down and emptied. I know there is fulness in God for such.

Sabbath 26th May

Dingwall 6.30pm. I took Jeremiah 31:3. 'Yea, I have loved thee with an everlasting love: therefore with lovingkindness have I drawn thee.' The everlasting love of God is the fountain from which our salvation springs. The consequences of being loved are that they are drawn to Christ, and inclined towards all that belongs to him. There were two ministers in front of me with about a hundred combined years of ministerial experience. I could only say what the Lord taught me.

Wednesday 29th May

Today I was doing a little painting about the place. Paint covers many a defect in wood, which may at heart be rotten. We should however praise God for the civility, courtesy, outward decency and the order of society which (in the main) have no inward regard for God. What mercies are in the world, all for the sake of the church! These were dearly purchased by the one to whom neither politeness nor kindness was shown by men who did not believe in him.

Friday 31st May

After various visits and tea at the National Hotel, I proceeded to the manse for the Kirk Session meeting. We agreed to protest to the parties responsible for opening a betting shop in Leopold Place.

Saturday 1st June

I feel the usual burden. I am sure there is enough in the fulness of Emmanuel, as the old pensioner sitting at the roadside said, 'Although I am empty, the King has plenty.' I can only wait upon him. May he prepare us all for the eternal Sabbath in heaven.

Friday 7th June

Shieldaig communion. The Question was given out by Angus MacInnes, Torridon, from Psalm 40:1–3. John Mackenzie said. 'It takes infinite power to take the soul from seeking righteousness by the law.' Hector Campbell spoke of a man who sheltered in a cave from a storm, but when the sun eventually shone through the roof of the cave he saw wild animals in it and hurried out. Seven spoke to the Question.

At 6pm Mr Campbell, Edinburgh,[249] preached on Psalm 68:13. 'Though ye have lien among the pots, yet shall ye be as the wings of a dove'. He said that Israel made no progress towards the Promised Land while the ark was stationary. He said that if we have the hope that we shall inherit the kingdom, let us not be highminded but fear. He spoke of a

---

[249] Donald Campbell (1908–1983) was pastor of Raasay from 1942 to 1947. He served Stornoway from 1947 until 1951 and then was minister of Edinburgh from 1951 until his death. His preaching was valued by exercised Christians and he was respected for his integrity. 'Obituary: The Rev. Donald Campbell, M.A., Edinburgh', *FPM* Vol. 92 (March 1987): pp. 76–82.

woman in Skye who had been down in spiritual depths, but soon afterwards was singing, 'For sure the Lord will not cast off / those that his people be.'[250]

Friday 14th June

Lochcarron communion. The Question was given out by J. Mackenzie in Colossians 1:13.[251] In opening it, Rev. John Nicolson (Ness)[252] said, 'One can never appreciate Christ until he finds out his inability to do anything to help himself.' Alex Maclean said that this people grieve for their shortcomings. Hector MacBeath[253] said: 'This people cannot stand [others] speaking ill of the ways of God.'

Thursday 20th June

Gairloch communion. At 6pm Rev. Fraser MacDonald preached from Zephaniah 3:2. 'She obeyed not the voice; she received not correction; she trusted not in the Lord; she drew not near to her God.' His points were as follows:

1. Who it is who makes the charges.

2. The charges made are fourfold—they received not correction, obeyed not, trusted not, and drew not near.

---

[250] Psalm 94:14, metrical version.

[251] 'Who hath delivered us from the power of darkness, and hath translated us into the kingdom of his dear Son.'

[252] John Nicolson (1919–1977) was born in Glasgow. He learned Gaelic and was ordained and inducted to the Ness (Isle of Lewis) congregation on 21st April 1964. In 1971 he accepted a call to Tain 1971 which he pastored until his death. 'Rev. John Nicholson, Tain', *FPM* Vol. 86 (January 1981): pp. 14–18.

[253] Mr MacBeath was born in September 1888 in Torgarve, Applecross, and died in February 1970. He was married to Johanna Maclennan who died in 1966. They lived in Killilan, a remote hamlet in Lochalsh.

Friday 21st June

Sandy Maclean gave out the Question in Isaiah 41:17.[254] Angus Macleod spoke of a horse which needed water and was brought to a well but would not bend its knees to reach down and drink. Roddy MacDonald[255] said that this people could say, 'Entreat me not to leave thee,' and 'Not unto us, Lord, not to us, / but do thou glory take.'[256] Hector MacBeath said that his brother in the trenches heard his father praying in Scotland. Mr Colquhoun concluded. He referred to wells in the Highlands where not a blade of grass was to be seen on the path leading to them, showing that the water was being used. Nine spoke to the Question.

Sabbath 23rd June

Gairloch communion. Rev. Colquhoun spoke from Song of Solomon 2:3 on 'the apple tree among the trees of the wood'. In his Table Address[257] he said, 'You have the hope that when the last messenger will come it will be to you a messenger of peace.'

At 6pm Rev. Fraser MacDonald spoke on the roll that was cut with a penknife and cast into the fire [Jeremiah 36:23]. He

---

[254] 'When the poor and needy seek water, and there is none, and their tongue faileth for thirst, I the Lord will hear them, I the God of Israel will not forsake them.'

[255] A prison officer at Barlinnie, Mr MacDonald belonged to North Uist, was an elder in Glasgow and latterly lived in Dingwall, where he was also an elder. 'Tribute to Mr Roderick Macdonald, Elder, Dingwall', *Synod Proceedings*, May 1992 (Glasgow, 1992), p. 15.

[256] Psalm 115:1, metrical version.

[257] Table Addresses are short devotional talks by a minister at the communion table, focussing communicants' thoughts on the dying love of the Saviour. Two are given: one just before and one immediately after the elements have been served.

said that many people cut the roll of the Word of God with the penknife of indifference.

Monday 24th June

Gairloch communion, Thanksgiving service. Rev. Colquhoun took Malachi 4:2. 'But unto you that fear my name shall the Sun of righteousness arise with healing in his wings.' He said that those who fear God's name would fear to offend God or his true people. Their prayer is, 'Hold up my goings.'[258] They fear for the cause of Christ in this evil day. They are not satisfied when Christ's cause is so low. They grow in knowledge of themselves and also in the knowledge of God's longsuffering. They grow in strength to witness for the Lord.

Thursday 27th June

Inverness communion. Rev. Malcolm MacSween (Oban) took the Pharisee and the publican from Luke 18. He said that the Pharisee was proud, uncharitable, had no confession of sin, was self-dependent, and thought that his sins were outbalanced by his virtues. The publican approached with reverence, fear and penitence.

Friday 28th June

Inverness communion. At 12 noon Rev. Alfred Mac-Donald took 1 Kings 14:6,[259] where Jeroboam's wife pretended to be someone else.

---

[258] Psalm 17:5, metrical version.
[259] 'And it was so, when Ahijah heard the sound of her feet, as she came in at the door, that he said, Come in, thou wife of Jeroboam; why feignest thou thyself to be another? for I am sent to thee with heavy tidings.'

At 6.30pm the Question was given out by Finlay Beaton in Ephesians 5:8.[260] Eight were called to speak.

Sabbath 30th June

Inverness communion. Rev. Alfred MacDonald took the Action Sermon, preaching on John 9:4. 'I must work the works of him that sent me, while it is day.' In fencing the Table[261] Mr MacDonald spoke of a man who came before a Kirk Session. While they were pleased with his knowledge, they told him he could not sit at the Lord's Table as they did not know his manner of life. The refused man then praised God that there was such a faithful Kirk Session in the land. Mr MacDonald debarred from the Lord's Table those who are not willing to give a bill of divorce to every sinful lust and passion which dwells in their heart. He invited to the Lord's Table those who mourn for their wholeness of heart and are afraid of it as well as those who look to Christ for everything.

---

[260] 'For ye were sometimes darkness, but now are ye light in the Lord: walk as children of light.'

[261] Fencing the Table is the part of the communion service where the minister explains who should, and who should not, partake of the Lord's Supper. He invites those who should come to the Table, by describing the evidences of conversion, to encourage them. On the other hand, in the name of the Head of the Church, he debars the rest, who have no Biblical right to partake of the Sacrament, by giving Scripture-based marks of those who are not the people of God. Portions of Scripture from Galatians 5:19–26 and Matthew 5:1–12 are usually read out. The practice can be traced to the New Testament and was emphasised under other descriptive names at the Reformation in documents such as Calvin's *Service Book* (1542) and *The Book of Common Order*, which was introduced to the English congregation in Geneva by John Knox in 1556, adopted by the Scottish Reformers in 1562, and revised in 1564. Later the practice was enjoined in the Westminster Assembly's *Directory for the Publick Worship of God* (1645).

Friday 5th July

Beauly communion. The Question was given out by John Maclennan in Acts 1:8. 'Ye shall be witnesses unto me.' It was opened by Mr MacAskill (Lochinver) who said that this people desire to fear God, and that they also witness for God by their conduct in the world. Twelve spoke to it.

Saturday 6th July

Beauly communion. Ephesians 2:10.[262] Rev. Donald Nicolson said that Paul thought at one time that nothing was right unless he had a hand in it.

Later Mr MacAskill (Lochinver) preached on Numbers 10:29[263] about Moses' invitation to Hobab. He said that all journeys must have a beginning. At the beginning of the spiritual journey, a sacrifice is required, just as in Egypt a lamb was killed, bringing before us 'the Lamb of God which taketh away the sin of the world'. It was a tonic to our souls to see two new members added to the church.[264] May the Lord hold up their goings.

---

[262] 'For we are his workmanship, created in Christ Jesus unto good works, which God hath before ordained that we should walk in them.'

[263] 'And Moses said unto Hobab, the son of Raguel the Midianite, Moses' father in law, We are journeying unto the place of which the Lord said, I will give it you: come thou with us, and we will do thee good: for the Lord hath spoken good concerning Israel.'

[264] One of these was Iain Graham. He married Rachel Sinclair (a sister of Rev. Robert R. Sinclair) and they had three children: twins James Stephen Sinclair and Marion Mackenzie, and Jane. Marion Graham died in 2008, having served for many years on the Church's Zimbabwe mission, latterly as head teacher of the John Tallach Secondary School. Iain Graham was ordained as an elder in 1972 and died in 1976.

Monday 15th July

'St Swithin's Day'. I often heard that if it rains on this day, it will rain on and off for six weeks. From my personal observation, I do not believe it is all superstition; I rather think there may be physical reasons for it. 'Yea, what is good the Lord will give.'[265]

Thursday 18th July

Daviot communion. At 12 noon Mr MacAskill (Lochinver) took Psalm 80:18.[266] He said that when God forsakes us, the fault is on our side. If a little error in the course of a ship is allowed to continue, it will be much in a few days.

At 7pm Mr McPherson took Job 34:31.[267] Job's brethren insisted there must be something in Job's life for which judgments came on him. We cannot grasp the immensity of the results of sin. There is an agreement between sin and misery. Job could not say that God gave him more than his sins deserved.

Friday 19th July

Daviot communion. A. McPherson gave out the Question in Song of Solomon 5:1.[268] It was opened by Mr MacAskill who quoted Rev. Donald Beaton saying, 'I came to see this scripture in a new light, namely forgiveness according to the riches of his grace.' Nine men spoke to the Question. It was

---

[265] Psalm 85:12, metrical version.

[266] 'So will not we go back from thee: quicken us, and we will call upon thy name.'

[267] 'Surely it is meet to be said unto God, I have borne chastisement, I will not offend any more.'

[268] 'I am come into my garden, my sister, my spouse: I have gathered my myrrh with my spice; I have eaten my honeycomb with my honey; I have drunk my wine with my milk: eat, O friends; drink, yea, drink abundantly, O beloved.'

closed by Rev. A. McPherson who said he thought it would be more useful to give marks of those who were a long time on the way, rather than marks of effectual calling.

Friday 26th July

I was cutting nettles in the evening. All this foul weed needs in order to thrive is to leave it alone; other crops such as potatoes and turnips thrive better by rousing and scraping around them. So we need spiritually to be mowing down the foul weeds which grow in our souls. 'Put away from you anger, wrath, malice, envy and evil speaking. Put off the old man with his corrupt lusts.'

Friday 2nd August

Dingwall communion. I gave out the Question in John 20:30–31.[269] I asked for marks of those taught by the Holy Spirit that the Scriptures are the only and all-sufficient means of salvation. Speaking in Gaelic, Angus Nicolson said he thought the Question was suitable but that he felt unfit to speak to it. He gave marks: they pray, they attend the means and the Lord's people are their companions. There were thirteen called to speak and a good few left out.

At 7pm Mr McPherson (Stratherrick) took Romans 15:4.[270] He said young converts may be regarding old believers in high estimation, but come later to see they are not what they thought them to be; in fact, they see them to be very

---

[269] 'And many other signs truly did Jesus in the presence of his disciples, which are not written in this book: but these are written, that ye might believe that Jesus is the Christ, the Son of God; and that believing ye might have life through his name.'

[270] 'For whatsoever things were written aforetime were written for our learning, that we through patience and comfort of the scriptures might have hope.'

faulty. They should not, however, despise their brethren. The comfort of believers is that Christ is the same.

Saturday 3rd August

Dingwall communion. Rev. D.M. MacLeod (Stornoway) took Luke 12:32. 'Fear not little flock.' He said we are liable to distrust God about temporal mercies and also about spiritual ones. God's flock are little in their own eyes, but Christ is great in their sight. You desire to love Christ because he died for you. You may feel cast down, in darkness, and saying, 'If God is with me how can I be like this?' Satan does not like to hear of Christ's blood. We had one new member.

Thursday 8th August

Portree communion. Mr MacAskill (Lochinver) took John 4:10.[271] He said that if a man has the knowledge of which Christ spoke to the woman at the well in Samaria, he is left in no doubt as to his sinful state.

Friday 9th August

Portree. The Question was given out by Alexander Nicolson (Glasgow) in Matthew 5:6. 'Blessed are they which do hunger and thirst after righteousness: for they shall be filled.' There were twenty-six on the list for speaking. Alex Beaton said that this people tasted of the sweetness of pardon. They love God's Word. They would like to be what they are not. They love secret prayer; I have good hope of such as have this exercise. Donald Mackay (Rona) said that one thing is true—once they did not have this thirst but were following after vanity. A day came in which they desired to follow Christ

---

[271] 'Jesus answered and said unto her, If thou knewest the gift of God, and who it is that saith to thee, Give me to drink; thou wouldest have asked of him, and he would have given thee living water.'

through good and ill report. They feel cold and dead, yet it is to the means of grace they go for refreshment. The house of God is the place they like best. They don't want to dwell in the tents of sin. They value the throne of grace to speak to the one who took their nature, as the child goes to his father. John MacLean (Raasay)[272] said their sense of emptiness is at its lowest ebb when supply is near. They thirst after knowledge. They thirst for their affections to be satisfied with the love of Christ. They thirst after holiness.

Sabbath 11th August

Applecross. At noon I took Hebrews 2:3[273] and at 6pm I took the verse we had at the Question in Portree, Matthew 5:6.

Thursday 15th August

Dingwall prayer meeting. Rev. D.A. Macfarlane. He took Luke 14:26. 'If any man come to me, and hate not his father, and mother, and wife, and children, and brethren, and sisters, yea, and his own life also, he cannot be my disciple.' Mr Macfarlane said, 'This is in a comparative sense. They are in this meeting who see Christ with many crowns on his head, as the one who hangs earth on nothing. If you are kissing the Son, the Father is pleased with you. You may be saying, "I'll be swamped if I don't get into the haven, Christ." If you desire the coming of Christ's kingdom and pray for your fellow men, your name is in the book of life.'

---

[272] Mr MacLean was missionary in Raasay from 1966 until 1970. He belonged to Northton, Isle of Harris. 'Mr John MacLean, Elder and Missionary, South Harris', *FPM* Vol. 93 (February 1988): pp. 56–57.
[273] 'How shall we escape, if we neglect so great salvation; which at the first began to be spoken by the Lord, and was confirmed unto us by them that heard him.'

Friday 16th August

Bonar Bridge communion. The Question was given out by D. Campbell[274] in 1 Peter 2:25.[275] We were at Professor Murray's house in Badbea for dinner. Professor Murray does not speak too much in private: it is very obvious that he is a profound thinker.

Wednesday 28th August

Ullapool. Rev. Alex MacAskill took the prayer meeting and preached in Psalm 106:3–4. 'Remember me, O Lord, with the favour that thou bearest unto thy people.' The Psalmist admits that God has a people in the world. It is strange that a vile sinner be allowed to ask God to visit them. What is 'the good of thy chosen'? It is the covenant of grace. This was David's comfort. Moses also refused the world to obtain it.

Thursday 29th August

Ullapool communion. At noon Rev. D. MacLean, Glasgow, took Mark 4:11–12. 'Unto you it is given to know the mystery of the kingdom of God.' We are born in a prison house. Our greatest concern should be: 'How can I be right with God?' How does a sinner have the truth fulfilled: 'Do thou with hyssop sprinkle me'? It is by faith in his blood. Then

---

[274] Donald Macfarlane Campbell (1903–1996) was raised in Eabost near Ose in Skye and later in the Bonar Bridge area. He was a missionary in Scourie and Kinlochbervie from the mid to late 1940s, and then in Kyle and Plockton until 1972, when he transferred to Bonar Bridge. 'Tribute to the late Mr Donald M. Campbell, Elder, Bonar Bridge', *Synod Proceedings, May 1996* (Glasgow, 1996), pp. 12–13. For his father, John Campbell, see 'The Late Mr John Campbell, Elder, Craigton, Bonarbridge', *FPM* Vol. 37 (September 1932): pp. 225–227.

[275] 'For ye were as sheep going astray; but are now returned unto the Shepherd and Bishop of your souls.'

peace of conscience will follow. Faith cannot be present without effectual calling. Regeneration and conversion are different. The moment a man looks to Christ by faith, he is out of prison and freed from condemnation.

Friday 30th August

Ullapool communion. The Question was given out by Angus Macleod. Romans 7:25. 'So then with the mind I myself serve the law of God; but with the flesh the law of sin.' Mr MacAskill (Lochinver) opened it, saying there are some things the believer can only tell to the Lord, not even to his wife. Abraham couldn't tell some things to Sarah. This people cannot tell others what they feel. They know nothing can cleanse them but the blood of Christ. They value the provision of the gospel. Eight were called to speak.

Wednesday 11th September

Ullapool, induction of Rev. Calum MacInnes.[276] Rev. Fraser MacDonald preached on Acts 20:24.[277] Points:

1. The ministry which Paul received. He said the ministry is the most honourable office on earth, but it entails labour, self-denial and devotion to duty.

---

[276] Mr Macinnes was raised in Cannich near Beauly. In 1957 he began work in the Dounreay nuclear power plant in Caithness. He professed faith in Halkirk. In 1968 he was ordained and inducted in Ullapool, where he ministered until 1973 when he accepted a call to London. In January 1977 he was inducted to Toronto, Canada. He joined the APC in 1989 and was translated to their Inverness congregation the next year. He retired in May 2010.

[277] 'But none of these things move me, neither count I my life dear unto myself, so that I might finish my course with joy, and the ministry, which I have received of the Lord Jesus, to testify the gospel of the grace of God.'

2. The manner in which he discharged it. He must have knowledge of himself. Paul wept many times; such is rare today. A minister should expect temptations. He must preach 'the whole counsel of God', not harping on one string only.

3. The results of his preaching: God was glorified. In the very place where they shouted themselves hoarse, shouting 'Great is Diana of the Ephesians', many were converted to Christ.

Wednesday 18th September

Inverness, Gaelic prayer meeting. John MacLeod, divinity student,[278] took Philippians 1:6.[279] Paul was taking no credit to himself. Lydia and the jailer were called but their experiences differed greatly. The work was to be carried along, little by little. They had to do their uttermost although salvation is of the Lord.

Wednesday 2nd October

Lochcarron communion. Rev. John Colquhoun took the prayer meeting. Psalm 55:22. 'Cast thy burden upon the Lord, and he shall sustain thee.' Those who are encouraged and invited are those made righteous by Christ's unspotted righteousness. Some of the burdens are: the question 'Had I a right beginning?'; the fear of offending God should be a burden;

---

[278] Harris-born Mr MacLeod was ordained and inducted on 30th December 1969 to the Stornoway congregation. He accepted a call to London in 2004 and remains there to the present date. He served as Clerk of Synod from 1995 to 2016, as well as tutoring divinity students in Greek and New Testament from 1981 to 1999, and Systematic Theology from 2002 to 2008.

[279] 'Being confident of this very thing, that he which hath begun a good work in you will perform it until the day of Jesus Christ.'

temptations and how ready we are to open the door to them; consciousness of inward corruptions; also a burden in connection with your profession. Are you as a congregation approaching a communion season without any burden? If so, there is something wrong. You may also have a burden in connection with your lot in providence, as referred to in the book *The Crook in the Lot*.[280] Paul had the thorn in the flesh. God promises to carry your burdens.

Thursday 17th October

Day of Prayer. Rev. D.A. Macfarlane took the service at noon from Psalm 2. The question is asked, 'Why do the heathen rage?' He gave examples of it: Goliath of Gath, Saul seeking David's life. He then came to New Testament times: the scribes and Pharisees raging against Christ, and Saul of Tarsus, were examples of heathenism. He took the phrase 'Kiss the son' and what was implied in it. One example was the late Rev. Donald Macfarlane (Raasay) tabling his protest in that vast [Free Church] assembly[281] and leaving a church which was unfaithful to Christ. So, what he and those who followed his example did was kissing the Son.

Sabbath 27th October

Raasay. At noon I took Luke 23:40–42. The thief on the cross went through steps which more or less every Christian goes through. He came to see his own demerit and sinfulness. He rebuked sin. He saw the deity of Christ. He began to pray.

At 5pm I took Revelation 22:14. 'Blessed are they that do his commandments, that they may have right to the tree of life.' The true believer sees in Christ one who spread himself

---

[280] By Thomas Boston of Ettrick.
[281] See Preface for Mr Macfarlane's separation from the Free Church.

along the vast dimensions of the holy, broad and spiritual law; and covered it all on behalf of his people.

Friday 15th November

Dornoch communion. The Question was given out by Donald Maclennan in John 9:25.[282] It was opened by Rev. Angus F. Mackay who said believers see the nature of sin, the riches of God's mercy, and also see that the work of grace must be done here.

Sabbath 17th November

Beauly 6pm. I took the text which had been the Question in Dornoch. I referred to a class of Christians for whom it is difficult to speak of the date of their conversion because of the manner of it being a gentle, gradual process. However, they are in no doubt as to what they see: their great sinfulness, the divinity of Jesus Christ, his offices as prophet and priest and king.

Saturday 14th November

Here I am carrying the usual burden. I cannot engage in anything with comfort on Saturday with this fear haunting me. The storehouse is in my hands, but I find it another matter to get anything out of it. All I can say is that I am casting my burdens on the Lord. He carries me through in my duties in a manner surprising to myself. The whole business is keeping me on my knees. I value the Holy Spirit above all else; I believe in God's good will toward me. I do not trust in any efforts to prepare for the Sabbath although I endeavour to do all I can. I cannot go to any door for help. I just wonder if any in a state of grace can feel so dead as I do.

---

[282] 'He answered and said, Whether he be a sinner or no, I know not: one thing I know, that, whereas I was blind, now I see.'

Tuesday 24th December

I heard the trade in 'Xmas' cards was 10% less in parts of England than in former years. I hope this trend will continue.

1969

Wednesday 1st January

At the service in Kilmorack at noon, I was led to Proverbs 3:5. 'Trust in the Lord with all thine heart; and lean not unto thine own understanding.' I observed that man will trust sooner to the creature than to God. We are greater idolaters than we are aware—worshipping the creature more than the creator—as the history of Israel shows.

1. We must have a knowledge of ourselves.

2. We must come to know God in Christ as he is revealed to us in the scriptures: a God of love, mercy, wisdom, power, and true to all his promises.

3. How this trust will manifest itself: the exercise of prayer, faith, patience (allowing God his time), and perseverance.

Friday 11th January

My wife and I visited Raigmore where we saw Mrs M. We prayed. I noticed a woman in the next bed dropped her cigarette and listened reverently. We never know what influence the Word and prayer may have. In any case, we should always do our duty, leaving the results with God.

Wednesday 22nd January

I took a circular tour through the wood about 5pm with two pots of marmalade. Left one at W's and the other at J's. After praying there, I came round the main road which resembled a suburb of a city more than the Highlands of Scotland, with traffic building up daily with the advent of the £30 million smelter at Invergordon.[283] I am very afraid with the influx of strangers to the north, that the effect morally and spiritually will inevitably be an adverse one. Sabbath work and traffic on the roads will considerably increase, incurring the displeasure of God, whatever the seeming prosperity and material gain. 'For what is a man profited, if he shall gain the whole world, and lose his own soul?' Matthew 16:26.

Thursday 23rd January

Inverness communion. Mr MacLean (Glasgow) and Rev. John Nicolson (Ness). Gaelic, Mr MacLean: John 1:48. Nathanael under the fig tree, from which he observed that sinners when converted desire secrecy [secret communion with God].

Friday 24th January

Question Meeting. Finlay Beaton gave out the Question from Romans 6:23. 'For the wages of sin is death; but the gift of God is eternal life through Jesus Christ our Lord.' Marks wanted of those who have the gift of eternal life, distinct from those who do not receive Christ and so are liable to the wages of sin. Nine were called to speak. There were forty-two on the list. That was not heard of before, as far as is known, in our church. Praise the Lord.

---

[283] Work on construction of an aluminium smelter began in 1968. It was in production from 1971 until British Aluminium closed it in 1981.

Saturday 25th January

Rev. D. MacLean. He spoke of the 'ivory palaces' in Psalm 45:8. One mark of those who love God: they hasten to the day of his coming. Ten members were added to the communion roll, eight of them coming to the Lord's Table for the first time.

Sabbath 26th January

Rev. D. MacLean took Isaiah 53:10. 'Yet it pleased the Lord to bruise him.' His points were:

1. The decrees of God, which shall stand.

2. One of the purposes of God in this decree—to make 'his soul' an offering for sin.

3. The fruit of the offering for sin.

He observed that Christ looked for comforters. He looked to the Jews, no comfort; to the disciples, no comfort; looked to the Romans, none; looked to heaven and it was closed on him. 'Comforters found I none.'

There were about 150 communicants.

Thursday 30th January

Dingwall communion. The morning Gaelic service was taken by Rev. John Angus MacDonald[284] in Luke 15:20.[285] When one is turned to God, he will seek retirement [solitude for prayer].

---

[284] Minister at Fort William. Harris-born Mr MacDonald (1910–1994) served previously in Uig (Lewis), Applecross and Raasay, and is remembered for his warm pastoral care. 'The late Rev. John Angus Macdonald', *FPM* Vol. 100 (May 1995): pp. 117–122.

[285] 'And he arose, and came to his father. But when he was yet a great way off, his father saw him, and had compassion, and ran, and fell on his neck, and kissed him.'

At the 12 noon English service, Mr MacLean [Glasgow] took Mark 4:11–12. He spoke of the solemn aspect of people failing to understand what they hear.

Friday 31st January

Dingwall communion. I gave out the Question in Psalm 51:1–2. In opening it, Mr MacDonald said there was very little of this soul exercise in the world today. John Mackenzie said, 'It is their sins that trouble this people.' Finlay Beaton said that the carnal mind keeps this people on their knees. It is the opposition within them to truth and holiness that troubles them. Sandy Maclean said they once had heard the Psalms with no effect. This people wonder if they ever prayed aright. Donald MacAskill: 'It is a great matter to come to this confession; although not guilty of adultery and murder as David was, yet they know these sins are in their heart.' Angus Macleod: 'This people cry for mercy for the way they despised the precious blood of Christ.' William Sim:[286] 'A mark: they never get the same taste off any human composition as they do of the Psalms.' Charlie Macleod: 'The fellowship meeting is useful as it reminds us of the duty of self-examination.' John MacLennan: 'This people are brought to know themselves.' Donald Mackenzie (Chapelton): 'This Psalm is honey to the people of God.' Seven ministers were present at the meeting.

Saturday 1st February

Dingwall communion. In Gaelic Rev. D. MacLean took Hebrews 11:3. 'These all died in faith.' Their faith was kept alive by the promises of God. The sign of being 'strangers and pilgrims' is that they do not feel at home in the world but

---

[286] Mr Sim lived in various places including Dingwall, Lairg and Dornoch. He died in Dingwall in February 1986. 'Mr William Sim, Elder', FPM Vol. 99 (November 1994): pp. 339–340.

quite at home in all that pertains to Christ and the things of the Spirit. Three new members. Praise the Lord.

Sabbath 2nd February

Dingwall. Mr MacDonald took the Action Sermon in Romans 4:25.[287] At the third table, Rev. D.A. Macfarlane said, 'I'll leave three passages with you: "The meek shall eat" from Psalm 22; "He giveth meat unto all those / that truly do him fear" [Psalm 111:5]; "Her food I'll greatly bless" in Psalm 132.'

Beauly 6pm. Mr MacDonald took Isaiah 38:5.[288] Hezekiah was given assurance that God heard him. God sees the tears of his people in this valley of tears. When God lengthens our days, we ought to make a right use of it.

Monday 3rd February

Rev. D. MacLean took Hebrews 12:27.[289] He gave the marks of growth in grace to consist of love to Christ as prophet, priest and king.

Monday 24th February

After visiting at Croy and Raigmore, my wife and I came to the Inverness prayer meeting. Finlay Beaton took it from Galatians 2:19.[290] I thought it was a good gospel discourse from

---

[287] 'Who was delivered for our offences, and was raised again for our justification.'

[288] 'Go, and say to Hezekiah, Thus saith the Lord, the God of David thy father, I have heard thy prayer, I have seen thy tears: behold, I will add unto thy days fifteen years.'

[289] 'And this word, Yet once more, signifieth the removing of those things that are shaken, as of things that are made, that those things which cannot be shaken may remain.'

[290] 'For I through the law am dead to the law, that I might live unto God.'

beginning to end. Eleneth Sutherland,[291] John Gunn and Finlay himself prayed.

Saturday 1st March

Ullapool communion. Rev. Calum MacInnes took the service from John 16:33.[292] He said we need law and gospel. If I remember rightly, there were twenty-nine intending communicants who remained for tokens.[293]

We were in Hector Campbell's for dinner, after which my wife and I returned to Tomich, arriving at 5pm. Praise the Lord for travelling mercies, our safety cometh from him. We found our habitation in peace, for which I desire to praise God for his restraining grace on my fellow creatures. God promised Israel of old that, when attending the feasts at Jerusalem, the heathen tribes would not invade them. I feel sure he can do the same yet for the spiritual Israel.

Sabbath 2nd March

Dingwall 6.30pm. I took the blowing of the Jubilee trumpet in Leviticus 25:9. It was good news to all who were in

---

[291] Eleneth Sutherland (1912–1997) was raised in Lairg where his father Charles Sutherland was a church missionary. Mr Sutherland professed faith in January 1962 in Inverness and was noted as being of 'a warm and bright disposition' and for being a 'balanced' Christian with a hospitable home. He was married twice: first to Frances Mackay of Rogart who died in 1972 and later to Chrissie Ferguson from Stornoway. 'Tribute to the late Mr Eleneth M. Sutherland, Elder, Inverness', *Synod Proceedings, May 1998* (Glasgow, 1998), p. 18.

[292] 'These things I have spoken unto you, that in me ye might have peace. In the world ye shall have tribulation: but be of good cheer; I have overcome the world.'

[293] A metal token issued to communicant members of churches in order to allow them entrance to the Lord's Supper.

bondage and poverty. I dealt with it as a type of the gospel trumpet, which is a joyful sound to all who realise their bondage to sin and Satan, and realise the poverty they are in through the fall; it is declaring to them that they can now be reinstated in the love and favour of the triune God.

Monday 3rd March

My wife and I were at Craig Dunain, visiting N. While there we saw the Apollo 9 blast-off for the moon with three men on board. It was most impressive.

Saturday 8th March

Margaret's funeral.[294] She died Thursday, aged 87. At 12 noon my wife, John and I left for Inverness, took Finlay Beaton across to the funeral service. It was conducted by Rev. Angus F. Mackay. I did not expect to see so many. Finlay Beaton opened with prayer, the portion read was Psalm 90, Mr Mackay praying at the end. Rev. William Grant gave the exhortation at the Mitchell Hill cemetery, Dingwall.

Wednesday 19th March

I read the tragic news of the loss of the Hoy lifeboat with all hands—eight of a crew.[295] My heart was sore reading the account of the upturned lifeboat towed to Thurso: a boat which saved six hundred lives.

Wednesday 26th March

My wife and I were up at Farley seeing old William Fraser, who is in his 87th year and living alone. We read in the Gaelic,

---

[294] Margaret was his sister.
[295] The Longhope lifeboat was lost on 17th March 1969 after answering a mayday call during one of the most severe storms in the islands.

which he preferred—there are very few in Kilmorack parish now of his kind who prefer Gaelic.

Wednesday 2nd April

London. Communion season. Rev. Alfred MacDonald took the prayer meeting. He took 'I am come that they might have life' (John 10:10). He said people were in danger of building on false delusive hopes for eternity.

Thursday 3rd April

London communion. Rev. Alfred MacDonald took the 11am service in Bridewell Hall.[296] He took Hosea 2:7. 'Then shall she say, I will go and return to my first husband; for then was it better with me than now.' He said, 'Those of you who are converted, you have not the sense of the love of God you once had.' He also said, 'God's people experience pain in connection with backsliding.' One pain they have is an absent Christ. Soul declension manifests itself in the neglect of prayer and a lack of delight in God's Word.

---

[296] The first designated Free Presbyterian service in London was conducted by Rev. James S. Sinclair (1867–1921) in St Andrew's Hall, 45 Palace Street, in December 1907. Rev. Neil Cameron took the second, in Eccleston Street Conference Hall (often shortened to Eccleston Hall) on 29th March 1908. From then, services continued there until February 1917. Between February and May 1917 the worshippers gathered in a hall at 109 Eaton Terrace. From May 1917 until April 1922 the venue was St Philip's Hall in Eccleston Place (later known as St Michael's Hall). Subsequently they used Eccleston Hall but after its destruction by fire in April 1956 they held services in Bridewell Hall for five months. From October 1956 until June 1974 the services took place in St Michael's Hall. Since 22nd June 1974 public worship has been held in the former Zoar Chapel in Varden Street, Whitechapel, which was purchased from the Gospel Standard Strict Baptists.

Friday 4th April

London communion. There was a service at St Michael's Hall at 11am, taken by Rev. A.F. Mackay. He took 1 Timothy 6:6. 'But godliness with contentment is great gain.'

1. He said that godliness consists in the indwelling of the Spirit, the recovery of the image of God in the soul, crucifying the flesh, warring against the corrupt nature, and saying, 'I have the seed of all sins within me.'

2. The fruit of godliness is contentment. He said that those who have it see no beauty in anything apart from Christ. They are satisfied with Christ, content with the will of God in grace and providence, bowing to his will in all things, well-contented with Christ and his salvation, and patiently waiting for the coming of Christ.

At 7pm the Question was given out by John Macdonald, Aldershot,[297] from John 9:35. 'Dost thou believe on the Son of God?' Those called were myself, Dennis Lewis,[298] Christian Puritz,[299] N. Miller[300] and Mr Miller senior.[301]

---

[297] Mr MacDonald was appointed as an elder in London in October 1966. He represented the congregation at Presbytery and Synod and moved to Greenock in the late 1970s.

[298] Dennis Lewis was an elder in the London congregation. He died in June 2005.

[299] Christian Puritz was born in Berlin in 1941, later studying mathematics at Oxford and Glasgow Universities in the 1960s. He taught mathematics for over 30 years in High Wycombe. Mr Puritz is the author of *Christ or Hitler?* (Darlington: Evangelical Press, 2013) and several school textbooks.

[300] Norman Miller originally belonged to the London congregation but after a period running a factory in Glasgow had served on the church's mission in Zimbabwe in the 1950s as a kraal schools supervisor assisting Rev. James Fraser (1913–1959).

[301] Mr Miller was once head waiter at the Savoy Hotel in London.

Friday 11th April

Fearn communion. The Question was given out by John Maclennan, Muir of Ord, in Romans 8:1.[302] Willie Sim mentioned three kinds of pride: pride of face, pride of race, and pride of grace.

Saturday 12th April

This is the 20th anniversary of our wedding day. I think the last twenty years have been the happiest time of my life. Such as wish to have a happy married life must be much in prayer and earnestly desire that they both will be praising God in heaven.

Wednesday 4th June

Shieldaig communion. Rev. Alfred MacDonald, Gairloch, took the prayer meeting. There was a baptism at the prayer meeting. The text was Genesis 17:26. 'In the self-same day was Abraham circumcised and his son Ishmael.' He observed that, by this, God was teaching men that there was something about us needing removal before we could worship him. It was a sign that we cannot worship God as we are, in our defilement. God in baptism confirmed that he had found a way.

Thursday 5th June

Rev. Malcolm MacSween (Oban) took the noon Gaelic service in Isaiah 66:2.[303] He spoke of the great privilege of this man that such a being as described here would look to him.

---

[302] 'There is therefore now no condemnation to them which are in Christ Jesus, who walk not after the flesh, but after the Spirit.'

[303] 'For all those things hath mine hand made, and all those things have been, saith the Lord; but to this man will I look, even to him that is poor and of a contrite spirit, and trembleth at my word.'

He is poor, has nothing, can do nothing. Why does he tremble at God's Word? Because he now believes all the threatenings will be fulfilled, because he sees Christ crucified for his sins. He will look to Christ in order to heal, cleanse and comfort him.

At 6pm Rev. Fraser MacDonald took Luke 23:39.[304] The other malefactor died impenitent. He was near to Christ but received no saving benefit from him.

Friday 6th June

Shieldaig communion. The Question was given out by Angus MacInnes, Torridon, in Luke 12:32.[305] Alex Nicolson said that this people seek holiness and are afraid of being left to themselves. Finlay Beaton said that this people know it is with God they have to do. They seek green pastures in the means of grace. They wonder at God's love, who went to the cross for them. He planted a grace in them for every grace in Christ.

Nine spoke to the Question. Rev. Fraser[306] [MacDonald] said he was surprised at how little the brethren dwelt on the fears of the Lord's people.[307]

Saturday 7th June

Shieldaig. Rev. Fraser took Acts 18:21.[308] He spoke of Paul's determination to keep the feast and that we should

---

[304] 'And one of the malefactors which were hanged railed on him, saying, If thou be Christ, save thyself and us.'

[305] 'Fear not, little flock; for it is your Father's good pleasure to give you the kingdom.'

[306] This is an example of an affectionate short form of a minister's name. Ministers would normally be addressed directly by their surname, e.g. 'Mr MacDonald'.

[307] Mr MacDonald gave this gentle ministerial rebuke as he closed the Question.

adopt Paul's motto: 'I must by all means keep this feast.' All under the blood of the Passover were equally safe, whatever their fears. The Passover meant that a sacrifice must die, and that the blood of the victim must be sprinkled. One hallmark of sincerity is a desire to keep all God's commandments.

Sabbath 8th June

Shieldaig communion. Mr MacSween preached a most sweet sermon on the words 'The next day John seeth Jesus coming unto him, and saith, Behold the Lamb of God, which taketh away the sin of the world' (John 1:29). I thought he had good liberty.

At 6pm Rev. Fraser preached on 'Is there yet any that is left of the house of Saul, that I may shew him kindness for Jonathan's sake?' (2 Samuel 9:1). He quoted Mr Gillies:[309] 'If you cannot come in by the door of the promises, you can come in by the door of the free offer.'

---

[308] 'But bade them farewell, saying, I must by all means keep this feast that cometh in Jerusalem: but I will return again unto you, if God will. And he sailed from Ephesus.'

[309] Malcolm Gillies (1885–1945) was born in Glasgow. His father was from Islay and his mother from Sandwick near Stornoway. He served as a missionary minister in Canada from 1920 to 1921, then as pastor of Halkirk from 1921 until accepting a call to Stornoway in 1925 where he laboured until his death. He was valued for his warm earnest preaching and diligent pastoral work, allied to personal kindliness to the poor. 'Tribute to the late Rev. Malcolm Gillies', *FPM* Vol. 50 (December 1945): pp. 141–144; 'Outer Isles Presbytery Tribute to Rev. M. Gillies', *FPM* Vol. 50 (January 1946): p. 176. A volume of Mr Gillies' sermons was published privately: *Fragments and Sermons of the Late Rev. Malcolm Gillies, Stornoway*, (Stornoway: n.p., 1987).

Monday 9th June

Shieldaig. Rev. MacSween preached from Psalm 46:4.[310] He said it was Luther's Psalm. Points:

1. He said a little about 'the city of God'. The city is the church, a place of safety. God defends it. The city is a place for buying and selling: 'Buy of me gold tried in the fire' to be rich for eternity. It is a place of privilege, such as we have in our own small denomination. Peace with God, the privilege of pardon. Peace of conscience. May God bring us to this city.

2. The river. God himself is the river, the Holy Spirit. 'Out of his belly shall flow' etc. What are the streams? They are the perfections of God. This is a wide subject. There is fulness in Christ to heal our diseases, and to give grace for grace. He spoke of the operations of the Spirit as the Comforter. The Holy Spirit is compared to water for cleansing. These streams make glad the city of our God. By contrast, earthly gladness is short-lived and will be drowned in eternal sorrow.

Thursday 19th June

Gairloch communion. At noon Rev. Donald MacLean (Glasgow) spoke of the leper who came to Jesus.

At 7pm Rev. Donald Campbell (Edinburgh) preached on the children of the promise. He said: 'Abraham when he got the promise laughed because it was so absurd. Abraham the man of God laughed at the idea of Sarah having a son.' I personally always thought it was a laugh of triumph, thinking of the power of God to accomplish anything.

---

[310] 'There is a river, the streams whereof shall make glad the city of God, the holy place of the tabernacles of the most High.'

Thursday 26th June

Inverness communion. Rev. Alex McPherson took Ecclesiastes 12:13.[311] He said, 'I noticed in Glasgow, in a well-to-do residential area, a group of aged women assembling every morning in a house for a coffee, in quest of happiness. I never saw people look so miserable. So, we see all is vanity.'

Friday 27th June

The Question at Inverness communion was given out by Ian Maclean[312] in Psalm 119:111.[313] Opening the Question Rev. Alex MacAskill, Lochinver, said that the soul is brought to see that the Word is powerful.

Saturday 28th June

Mr McPherson took Ephesians 4:30. 'And grieve not the holy Spirit of God, whereby ye are sealed unto the day of redemption.' The Spirit is grieved when we do not benefit by being afflicted, or by neglecting public profession when you hope Christ has redeemed you. Marks of sealing: Jesus is becoming sweeter to you, the soul is taught conformity to the pattern of Scripture in daily walk and dress, the soul is taught to leave himself at God's disposal, they desire spiritual prosperity, censure their fellow men less, and put a more favourable construction on their doings.

---

[311] 'Let us hear the conclusion of the whole matter: Fear God, and keep his commandments: for this is the whole duty of man.'

[312] Mr Maclean has held the office of elder in the Inverness congregation since 1962. He worked in the Inverness ironmonger Gilbert Ross, later running their Invergordon shop. Latterly he was manager of Farm & Household Stores in Inverness.

[313] 'Thy testimonies have I taken as an heritage for ever: for they are the rejoicing of my heart.'

Thursday 3rd July

Beauly communion. In English at 7pm, Rev. John Colquhoun (Glendale) preached on Hebrews 4:16. 'Let us therefore come boldly unto the throne of grace.'

1. The throne of grace. He spoke of the Old Testament Scriptures typifying Christ, dealing with men at the mercy seat. He is dealing with us now through the Scriptures, prayer and preaching.

2. The manner of coming—with boldness. There may be unholy boldness. We must come as such as have nothing, can do nothing, and are humbled because of our sins. The reasons why a soul comes with boldness are: one is satisfied with Christ, peace is ruling in his conscience, and one believes God will be faithful to his promises.

3. The end for which we are to come—to find mercy. Mercy is consistent with justice because God encourages him to come. We must come like the publican. When you are fully sanctified, your place in heaven will be ready for you.

Friday 4th July

Beauly communion. I gave out the Question in Isaiah 66:1–2.[314] It was opened by Mr Colquhoun who quoted Dr Kennedy's reference to those on the 'poor list'—they had nothing, could not work, and had no friends that could help them. Finlay Beaton said that it was a mark of this people that they know God is a consuming fire. They search the Scrip-

---

[314] 'Thus saith the Lord, The heaven is my throne, and the earth is my footstool: where is the house that ye build unto me? and where is the place of my rest? For all those things hath mine hand made, and all those things have been, saith the LORD: but to this man will I look, even to him that is poor and of a contrite spirit, and trembleth at my word.'

tures to see how they stand. They feel their need of a mediator. He quoted the man who said he found Christ in the manger wrapped in the swaddling clothes of the promises. He said they feel at home in spiritual conversation. They love to listen to the Word. They desire readiness for the heavenly country. John Mackenzie said he never got so much trembling at the Word as he would have wished.

Saturday 5th July

Rev. D.A. Macfarlane took Psalm 110:7. 'He shall drink of the brook in the way: therefore shall he lift up the head.' Mr Macfarlane said that divines differ as to what drinking of the brook means, but that he would give his own personal view, with some examples. It means drinking in the Word of God, its promises and its curses. One example was when Satan tempted Christ to turn stones into bread. Christ met him with the Word of God. Satan tried to drive a wedge between the will of Christ as man and the will of God. Drinking means to be in heart harmony with the Scriptures. Another example— when he stood up to read in the synagogue at Nazareth. Drinking of the brook means Christ is always acquiescing in the will of God, always pleased with the will of the Father. Another example is Psalm 22. Christ fulfilled the meaning of the Psalm. On the way to Emmaus, he in effect told them to drink out of the law and the prophets. Christ knew he would lift up his head—rise again on the third day.

Sabbath 6th July

Beauly communion. Rev. John Colquhoun took Song of Solomon 3:11. 'Go forth, O ye daughters of Zion, and behold king Solomon with the crown wherewith his mother crowned him in the day of his espousals, and in the day of the gladness of his heart.' The daughters of Zion are called such because they were born there and registered there. They were convinced of sin: it became a burden to them. What are they to do? They are to 'go forth'. Where from? Out of themselves. We are very self-centred and need to cease from creature help. Go forth out of duties, out of church-going and out of our prayer and privileges. Where to? To the family altar, means of grace, and to the sacraments, although afraid of them. Go forth in dependence on God, seeking his glory. What do they behold? King Solomon, the glorious king. The kingdoms of earth rise and fall. This kingdom of the New Testament Solomon will ever stand. King Solomon was noted for his wisdom—Christ builds his spiritual temple by infinite wisdom. They are to view Solomon in the 'day of his espousals'. The day of his espousals will give great pleasure to the true believer.

Monday 7th July

Beauly communion ends. Rev. Colquhoun took Psalm 29 in the Gaelic.

In English Rev. Alfred [MacDonald] took Matthew 13:14–15. This people had sufficient means at their disposal to let them see. It was expected of this people to see their privilege, their sins, and their condition.

Thursday 10th July

Tain communion. Rev. Donald MacLean preached in Luke 5:23–24. The healing of the sick of the palsy. He said that carrying his couch would remind the man of his sins. The true believer will be carrying his couch until he reaches home to his Father's house.

Sabbath 27th July

Beauly 12 noon. Joshua 1:1–2.[315]

1. Something about Moses now being dead. This shows that no person is indispensible and that God can find men to carry on his work when his servants are called home.

2. Let us notice Moses as representing the law, which will never bring any into heaven. Joshua, 'Saviour', represents the gospel. It was he who was appointed to bring Israel into Canaan. It is Christ alone who will bring the spiritual Israel into the heavenly Canaan.

3. A little about the Jordan drying up before the Ark of the Covenant as a type of Christ making the Jordan of death a safe passage to glory for the Israel of God.

Friday 1st August

Dingwall communion. I gave out the Question in John 17:16, 'They are not of the world as I am not of the world.' Thirteen men spoke. Finlay Beaton said, 'This people say, "I'll hear what God the Lord will speak." This people went to the covenant of works first. They feel an evil heart of unbelief. They have a hope they will never be put to shame. They cannot do without the blood. It is to a reconciled God in Christ they look. This people have many ups and downs. They see the mercy of God in bearing with them. They desire a heart knowledge—Christ is made to them wisdom' [1 Corinthians 1:30].

---

[315] 'Now after the death of Moses the servant of the Lord it came to pass, that the Lord spake unto Joshua the son of Nun, Moses' minister, saying, Moses my servant is dead; now therefore arise, go over this Jordan, thou, and all this people, unto the land which I do give to them, even to the children of Israel.'

Saturday 2nd August

Rev. D.B. MacLeod took Matthew 28:5.[316] There was one new member.

John Mackenzie of Kishorn took the 6pm prayer meeting. I never saw so many at the prayer meeting.

Wednesday 6th August

I left for Portree, arriving there about 4pm, where I was met by Calum Gillies[317] who took me to his house.

Thursday 7th August

Portree communion. At noon Rev. Malcolm MacSween (Oban) took the parable of the Pharisee and the publican. There was a difference between them in the fruits of their prayers, namely one was justified and the other under condemnation. The Pharisee had cause to thank God for his restraining grace, but he was proud of his attainments. His prayer was more a song of self-praise.

Tuesday 12th August

Bill Byers[318] and I left Portree at 9.30am. I was taken to see Donald MacAskill in Portnalong,[319] then a school teacher Miss

---

[316] 'And the angel answered and said unto the women, Fear not ye: for I know that ye seek Jesus, which was crucified.'

[317] Calum Gillies (1925–1997), originally from Raasay, was a Portree shopkeeper and regular precentor in the local congregation. He was brother to Alasdair Gillies (1923–1999), an elder in Glasgow—see footnote for 23rd March 1970.

[318] Bill Byers (1933–2017) was a well-known elder. He and his wife Marion lived in Dunvegan, Ayrshire, Portree, Inverness and later in Easter Ross and South Queensferry. 'William MacAngus Byers', *The Door* (Spring 2018): pp. 6–9. He was a grandson of William MacAngus, Fearn—see footnote for 7th September 1957.

Mary MacInnes who was teaching in Rona 49 years ago. We went into Dunvegan and had afternoon tea with John Mackay.[320]

Thursday 4th September

Ullapool communion. At 6pm Rev. D.B. MacLeod took Mark 10:21 on the rich young ruler. The points made were as follows:

1. This man concerned himself with eternal life. He was different to the multitude around Christ at this time. He was earnest in the matter, and confessed he needed instruction. He also led an upright life. He kept the law outwardly. Christ approved of what he saw in him and loved him with a love of complacency.

2. The test his religion was put to was to go and sell all that he had. God never gave an unreasonable command. He saw fit to apply this test to him. Notice, however, that Christ promised him better riches.

3. 'Take up thy cross.' The Christian life calls for self-denial. Christ showed the man where he stood—the love of the world came between him and God. Christ also said that only God was good. Carnal men would rest in this world rather than strive after the rest of heaven. We do not require great riches to keep us from Christ; it depends on whether your heart is clinging to it.

---

[319] Mr MacAskill lived in Fernilea, Carbost. He was an elder in the Bracadale congregation. He died in October 1990. A contemporary of Alasdair Beaton, Struan, (1892–1980), he supplied other congregations, particularly Staffin.

[320] Mr Mackay was an elder in Skye, who died in 1975. He ran a shop in Dunvegan with his brother Neil. Their sister Janet lived with them.

Friday 5th September

The Question in Ullapool was given out by Hector Campbell in Psalm 51:10. 'Create in me a clean heart.' Sandy Maclean said that this people mourn for the time they spent in the service of Satan. They also admire God's patience in bearing with them. The lamb, which at first would not look at the food the others had, when it tasted of it would run for it. They desire to give glory to God, weak and backward as they feel. They desire that he would fill their hearts.

Tuesday 9th September

I was collecting the Sustentation Fund[321] and visited four houses. I found an old man and woman (whose combined ages would make about 170 years) reading the Bible at 5pm. Do you know, it impressed me (in this age of hurry-scurry when the Bible is regarded as out of date just like an old calendar) to find people engaged in this exercise. May the Lord bless to them thus honouring his Word.

Saturday 13th September

The boat left Kyle for Applecross and about an hour or so later we arrived at Toscaig pier. There would be about ten passengers. Mrs Murray[322] met me.

---

[321] A fund begun by the Disruption 'father', Dr Thomas Chalmers (1788–1847). It specifically supports minister's salaries. Prior to the envelope system for distinguishing contributions made at the church door, collectors of the Fund used to visit the homes of people who wished to contribute.

[322] The minister's wife, Mrs Marjory Murray (née Graham). She died on 30th August 2015. Her husband, Rev. Alexander Murray was born in 1925 at Aultnagar, Sutherland. He was licensed in August 1953 and ordained in February 1954. He served in Winnipeg, Canada from 1954 to 1956 (with further short visits in 1969 and 1979). He was pastor of Applecross from 1956 to 1984 and he then served

Sabbath 14th September

Supplied Applecross. The morning service was in Gaelic and in English. I took Matthew 7 about the wise man who built his house on a rock. There were approximately forty to fifty present.

At 6pm the service was in English and I took John 10:9.[323]

Monday 15th September

Applecross. I was visiting at Camustiel in the morning and prayed in six houses, indifferent as to what church they were of.

Tuesday 16th September

Applecross. Mrs Murray kindly drove me to Milltown in the morning. I prayed in five houses, arriving back at the manse about 1pm for lunch. I spent the afternoon reading. After tea Mrs Murray and I went to Culduie. I visited three houses where I prayed. My last call was on the elder, Colin Gillies, with whom we had worship.[324]

Wednesday 8th October

Gairloch communion. We left for Opinan about 6.30pm. Rev. Alex MacAskill (Lochinver) preached in the new meeting house from Colossians 2:9. 'For in him dwelleth all the fulness of the Godhead bodily.' He spoke of the fulness of

---

in the Lairg-Bonar-Dornoch-Rogart joint charge from 1984 until 1989. The joint charge was formed in 1983; Helmsdale was added later. Mr Murray joined the APC in 1989.

[323] 'I am the door: by me if any man enter in, he shall be saved, and shall go in and out, and find pasture.'

[324] Colin Gillies (c.1894–1975) of No. 9 Culduie was a fisherman. He was married to Jessie MacAulay, who died in 1977. Jessie was a daughter of John MacAulay a famous missionary in Applecross and Lochalsh.

power, fulness of light, fulness of life, and the fulness of love that is in Christ. I liked the discourse very well. (I was impressed at the elaborate place of worship the Laide boys erected—a lovely pulpit and precentor's enclosure.)[325]

Thursday 9th October

Gairloch communion. At noon, Mr MacAskill took Ezekiel 33:11.[326] His points were:

1. That God has no pleasure in the destruction of the wicked.

2. What God hath pleasure in.

3. The exhortation 'Turn ye, why will ye die?'

At 6pm Rev. Alex Morrison (North Uist)[327] preached on Paul's address to King Agrippa in Acts 26.

1. His first point was the importance of repentance, and how it is insisted on by both the Old and New Testament authors.

2. His second point was a few things implied in repentance—we have strayed from God, come short of his law, and are condemned already except we repent.

3. His third point was the nature of repentance. You have it in the Prodigal Son. All believers are not alike, but they agreed in saying that they sinned against heaven and are not worthy of being his son. He said, 'Don't think

---

[325] The 'Laide boys' were the contractors Macrae Brothers Ltd, based in the village of that name.

[326] 'Say unto them, As I live, saith the Lord God, I have no pleasure in the death of the wicked; but that the wicked turn from his way and live: turn ye, turn ye from your evil ways; for why will ye die, O house of Israel?'

[327] Alexander Morrison (1925–1999) was from Ness in the Isle of Lewis. Respected for theological ability, he served as pastor of North Uist from 1959 to 1999. 'The Late Rev Alexander Morrison', *FPM* Vol. 104 (November 1999): pp. 330–334.

because you have terrors that you have repentance, which consists of turning unto God.'

Friday 10th October

Gairloch communion. The Question was given out by Hector MacLeod[328] in Zephaniah 3:12. 'I will also leave in the midst of thee an afflicted and poor people, and they shall trust in the name of the Lord.' Seven or eight spoke to it. Sandy Maclean said that Psalm 115, which had already been quoted, was true—they seek not to glory in themselves; they put the crown of their salvation on the head of Christ.

At 7pm Mr MacAskill spoke from Numbers about the passover. The people journeying after the passover could not have been part of the church while kept as slaves by Pharaoh. He also spoke of how they were freed. They had to find a lamb—so must we find the Lamb of God if we are to be freed. They had to kill the lamb; God in our nature had to die. Blood had to be put on the lintels, there was no deliverance without this.

---

[328] Hector Macleod was an elder in the Gairloch congregation. He served in the 51st (Highland) Infantry Division during the Second World War and was captured by the Germans at St Valéry-en-Caux, France. He remained a Prisoner of War until peace in 1945. It is said that it was clear afterwards that he had had 'rich spiritual experiences' in the PoW camp. He is remembered as having 'rare spiritual gifts', with a great sense of the majesty of God, and of the need of the blood of the Lamb in approaching the Most High. 'He seems to have had a high degree of assurance of personal salvation even when fighting with unbelief and corruption within his own soul. However, his assurance was of a lower degree during his last illness, but he was enabled to meditate more in his final week of life on the sufferings of Christ than upon his own severe pain.' 'The Late Hector MacLeod, Elder, Gairloch', *FPM* Vol. 100 (March 1995): pp. 83–86.

Sabbath 12th October

Gairloch communion. Mr MacAskill preached on Song of Solomon 2:8. 'The voice of my beloved! behold, he cometh leaping upon the mountains, skipping upon the hills.'

Thursday 23rd October

Beauly prayer meeting. Twenty-eight people attended. I took Matthew 14:23 about Peter meeting Christ walking on the water. Christ's time in coming is always the best, as in the case of Lazarus and Jairus. Christ usually sends relief when men are ready to appreciate it. The sinner must be humbled before he is ready to value Christ.

Thursday 13th November

Harvest Thanksgiving Day. Rev. D.A. Macfarlane spoke in John 4:29 about the woman of Samaria who said, 'Come, see a man, which told me all things that ever I did.' Without any heads of sermon, Mr Macfarlane kept on without a stop where an ordinary man would get lost, speaking of the manner in which Christ dealt with the woman. He asked, 'What has this to do with thanksgiving? It is the backbone of the matter: Christ is the procuring cause of all lesser mercies.'

Friday 14th November

Dornoch communion. The Question was given out by Donald Maclennan in Joshua 24:15. 'As for me and my house we will serve the Lord.' William Sim quoted the late Rev. Neil Cameron to the effect that the petition 'Restore me thy salvation's joy' shows that they had a taste of it already. Donald Campbell gave a mark of grace that they have no confidence in their service for Christ. John Maclennan quoted Mary Macphail saying, 'O how I love the Holy Spirit!' He gave the following marks: they are ashamed of themselves and afraid of themselves. Iain Mackenzie gave two marks of grace: they have fellowship with his people, and they know that all their mercies are from God. Eight men spoke to the Question.

Sabbath 30th November

At noon in Dingwall I took Mary and Martha in Luke 10. I observed that these two women represented two classes of true Christians—one excitable, hasty, and inclined to fault-finding; the other one pious, gentle, clothed with humility, of a teachable nature and loveable.

Beauly 6pm. My wife complained in the afternoon that I had not spoken of Mary sitting at Christ's feet, so I decided to take the same portion tonight in Beauly. I observed that sitting at Christ's feet implied humility, a teachable disposition, and bearing the marks of discipleship. These marks are self-denial, bearing one's cross and following Christ, seeking to drink in his temper and disposition.

Sabbath 14th December

We worshipped in the new church in Beauly.

Sabbath 21st December

I was unwell and not out in church. John took the services in Beauly all day. At worship later we read the last two chapters of the Old Testament. 'The day cometh that shall burn like an oven.' This chapter is indelibly in my mind since childhood days because our father usually took Malachi 4 at worship when he was pressed for time, such as when the boat for Portree was waiting for him. In that chapter the fate of the righteous and the wicked is clearly set forth. The last words of the Old Testament end with a curse, while the New Testament ends with 'the grace of the Lord Jesus Christ'.

1970

Thursday 1st January

Prayer Meeting, Beauly. I took Hebrews 13:8. 'Jesus Christ the same yesterday, and today and for ever.' I observed the dignity of his person, the extent of his power, the efficacy of his blood, the merits of his atoning death and his constant intercession. The very one that poor creatures, changeable as we are, need in a changing world: a lasting portion.

Sabbath 4th January

Mrs Macfarlane came for John about 11am, as the minister took a weak turn this morning.

Friday 9th January

We called at Dingwall manse where I read in the minister's bedroom, sang in Psalm 130, read in John 14. The minister prayed. He seemed burdened with the 'body of sin and death'. What a prayer!

Monday 12th January

My wife and I left for Inverness and visited M in hospital. Alas, she could not speak although she seemed to grasp who we were. When I said goodbye, she made an effort to give me her hand, which I am afraid will be the last time I see her. We then attended the prayer meeting. Mr Mackay took Philippians 1:21. 'For to me to live is Christ, and to die is gain', which I feel sure is applicable to the one we visited.

Friday 16th January

At Tain. We called on Archie Robertson, where I prayed. He was having a day in bed as advised by the doctor. He referred to John Cameron saying at Dingwall station, 'Joseph and Mary lost Jesus among their friends.' Several of the communion people had been assembled there on their way home.

Sabbath 18th January

In Dingwall at 6.30pm I took the parable of the fig tree from Luke 13. What does the digging and dunging imply? It may mean all God's dispensations by his Word, Spirit and providences calling men off from their sinful ways; knocking at their door with various trials either in soul, body or circumstances—losses, crosses and disappointments. I also spoke about the awful fate of those who bear no fruit after all God's dealings—namely, they are cut down as cumberers of the ground, bearing not the fruits of repentance, faith, love and new obedience.

Thursday 22nd January

Inverness communion. At 7pm Rev. Fraser MacDonald took 2 Timothy 2:11–13. There are two things here in particular:

    1. The sin of denying God.
    2. The awful result he will deny us.

We deny God when we don't ascribe to Christ the attributes of Deity, when our life and profession do not agree, when the commandments are broken and when you are afraid of incurring loss in witnessing for Christ.

Friday 23rd January

Inverness communion. At 6.30pm the Question was given out by John Gunn in John 9:25. 'One thing I know, that, whereas I was blind, now I see.' About eight or nine spoke.

In the morning Rev. Fraser MacDonald had preached in Exodus 32:26 on 'Who is on the Lord's side?' Those who have grace bear visible marks. There were some outstanding sins which brought Israel to the condition they were in—impatience, ingratitude and idolatry. It is a good mark if you can say, 'Thy kingdom come.'

Thursday 29th January

Dingwall communion. Rev. Donald Campbell (Edinburgh) preached on John 8:34. 'Whosoever committeth sin is the servant of sin'. He said that the word 'servant' here means 'slave'. He added that such was the power of sin that, if it were possible for a man addicted to drink to get out of hell, he would go again to the public house. God is offering to us today freedom from the power of sin.

Beauly 7pm. Rev. Donald MacLean (Glasgow) took Ezekiel 47:6. He said that God's people have an influence on the communities in which they live, like the healing waters.

Friday 30th January

Dingwall communion. I gave out the Question in John 17:3. 'And this is life eternal, that they might know thee the only true God, and Jesus Christ, whom thou hast sent.' Finlay Beaton gave as marks of grace that they are more concerned with the inner man than the outer man, take God's Word as their rule, and thank God for the gift of his Son. John Gunn said that Calvary is the hope of all of this people. Alex Maclennan, Diabeg, said it is the desire of this people to have what is in this portion of Scripture. Sandy Maclean, John Mackenzie, D. Campbell, Ian MacLeod,[329] Willie Sim, Ian Matheson,[330] D. MacAskill, Cameron Tallach[331] and Donald Mackenzie (Chapelton) spoke.

Saturday 31st January

Dingwall communion. Mr Macfarlane took the English service in Romans 7:4.[332] 'May he give us a spoonful of fear of his holy name,' he said.

Sabbath 1st February

Dingwall communion. Mr Campbell (Edinburgh) took Luke 23:46.[333] He said, 'Your sins were in the cup he drank if you are honest in commemorating his death.'

---

[329] Born in Fearn, Mr Macleod (1923–2001) was a policeman who served as an elder in Dornoch, then Dingwall. 'The late Mr Ian M. Macleod, Elder, Dingwall', *FPM* Vol. 106 (August 2001): pp. 245–248.

[330] Mr Matheson was an elder in Fort William. He was a son of the Dingwall elder, Kenneth Matheson (see footnote 50).

[331] At this time Cameron Tallach was working as a doctor in Scotland, but had a sense of calling to work in the Far East. He and his wife Ishbel (née Maclean) later moved to Taiwan, and then to Hong Kong, where they undertook medical missionary work among Chinese people for almost 30 years.

[332] 'Wherefore, my brethren, ye also are become dead to the law by the body of Christ; that ye should be married to another, even to him who is raised from the dead, that we should bring forth fruit unto God.'

[333] 'And when Jesus had cried with a loud voice, he said, Father, into thy hands I commend my spirit: and having said thus, he gave up the ghost.'

Tuesday 10th February

My wife and I left for Tain at noon, took our dinner there, and then we visited Archie Robertson. He was in bed but quite lively. He told me that Self was becoming his greatest enemy, something he had been a stranger to in his early years. He spoke largely of how this enemy robs God by giving glory to the creature.

Thursday 26th February

Ullapool communion. Rev. John MacLeod (Stornoway) took Exodus 5:2. 'Who is the Lord that I should obey him?' His points were:

1. Our duty in relation to the question.
2. The question reveals our character.
3. How the question was answered in the experience of Pharaoh.

Thursday 5th March

Beauly prayer meeting was attended by about twenty-four people. I took Romans 2:28. 'For he is not a Jew, which is one outwardly.' There were those in every age who are Jews outwardly and those who are Jews inwardly. It shows profound ignorance of ourselves, of God's nature, and of the spirituality of God's law, to rest on outward performances. We should seek to be through and through what we profess to be. The Christian who is one inwardly aims at spiritual, internal worship in all he does.

Tuesday 10th March

My sister May Dougan is staying with us. At May's request, Rev. D.A. Macfarlane came across. We sang in Psalm 73 and he read in 2 Corinthians 5. The man of God made a lovely prayer.

Thursday 12th March

Beauly prayer meeting was attended by twenty-two peo-ple. I took Romans 10:4.[334] Ian MacDonald sang, giving out the line to the tune Ballerma. I seldom ever heard any of the older men take that tune, giving out the line.

Monday 23rd March

I left for Glasgow at 11.25. I arrived at Bentinck Street[335] about 4pm. Praise the Lord for travelling mercies.

Tuesday 24th March

I passed a pleasant time today with Tommy Macrae at Circus Drive.[336] He is one of the few remaining links with the past.

Wednesday 25th March

Left for London. I left Central Station, Glasgow at 10.12am. The train was not too full. I went for lunch, partly to pass the time. It was a nice break and cost me 18 shillings.

------

[334] 'For Christ is the end of the law for righteousness to every one that believeth.'

[335] The home of Alasdair Gillies (1923–1999) and his wife Katie (née Macleod). A teacher of English, who belonged to Raasay, he often held services. He served as an elder in Glasgow, and after his retiral north, in Dingwall. The couple were known for 'unstinting hospital-ity' and 'profitable conversation'. 'The late Mr Alasdair Gillies, Dingwall', *FPM* Vol. 105 (June 2000): pp. 177–180.

[336] Raasay-born Thomas MacRae died in Dumbarton in 1993. He became a communicant in Glasgow in 1933 and an elder there in 1946. 'Tribute to the late Mr Thomas MacRae, Elder, Dumbarton', *Synod Proceedings, May 1994* (Glasgow, 1994), p. 16.

Friday 27th March

London communion. John MacDonald, Aldershot, gave out the Question in Matthew 15, which refers to the woman of Canaan whose daughter was vexed grievously with a devil. Only four men were called to speak, out of the eight or nine who could have been. Rev. Lachie MacLeod[337] closed the Question and said that the woman accepted all that was said about her, yet she would not leave Christ. The only argument that believers use at a throne of grace is Christ and Calvary.

Tuesday 31st March

London Zoo. Alasdair Gillies and I went to the zoo about 11am. What a sight! Wild beasts from all quarters of the globe, also venomous reptiles. It was impressive to hear the lion roaring. The reptile house was very impressive. I was thinking how dreadful if all these reptiles were let loose on one. Man's heart is by nature a cage of such creatures. How the sight of these venomous creatures should make us flee to Christ to be saved from all that is within us, namely from our sins. Those taught from heaven are taught that their hearts are a stronghold of devils, a cage of every unclean and hateful bird. May we praise God for the one who has conquered all the hosts of hell for all who trust in him, love and serve him, and who will preserve them safely to his kingdom and glory.

Wednesday 1st April

London prayer meeting. Bridewell Hall. About thirty-five attended. I spoke on the Pharisee and the publican from Luke 18. The publican prayed to the right quarter—God in

---

[337] In the Highlands, Lachie is a shortened affectionate form of Lachlan.

Christ. He prayed for mercy, not for justice. He prayed as a sinner.

Monday 6th April

London. I did some visiting. M invited me for tea, after which we had worship. She loves to speak of olden times and the godly men she used to hear. I would rather her to speak more of Christ and the way of salvation. You cannot comfort her. At times she says, 'There is no mercy for me.' I consider this an unwise remark for one to make when God is offering mercy to them.

Friday 10th April

Fearn communion. The Question was given out by John Maclennan in Ephesians 2:1.[338] About six spoke to it. There were three more who could have been called. It was rare to have so many to speak on Friday in a small place.

Tuesday 14th April

We called on Donald Campbell, Free Church missionary at Beauly.[339] He is an exercised Christian. He has the spiritual mind which is so rare today. His company is edifying. If you should wonder at me visiting a Free Church man, my answer would be that I am happy to meet with those who belong to the 'church of the firstborn whose names are written in heaven', regardless of denomination. We may idolise our denomination. We should rather value personal piety and the image of

---

[338] 'And you hath he quickened, who were dead in trespasses and sins.'

[339] Donald Campbell (1899–1991) and his wife Effie (1904–1996) lived in Beauly from 1965 until 1987. He was from Ness, Lewis, and she from Staffin, Skye. They then moved to Achmore, Lewis to live with their daughter Mary Ann Macinnes.

Christ wherever we meet with it. This is not saying but I know where I stand.

Sabbath 19th April

At 6pm in Beauly I took 1 Corinthians 13:13. 'And now abideth faith, hope, charity.' Love will remain the only grace which will enter triumphant into heaven.

Tuesday 21st April

My wife, John and I left at 10.30am for our cousin's funeral from Chisholm's Funeral Home on George Street. It was Rev. D who kept the service, in which I did not hear a word of caution regarding preparation for death, no word about sin. It was all smooth sentences, collecting promises from various places in Scripture. No word about the need for holiness and meetness for heaven. I am afraid he was a 'blind leader of the blind'. Such are the times on which we have fallen.

Monday 27th April

After the prayer meeting my wife arrived with the news that my sister May had passed on. She and I were close companions in youth. I have the hope she arrived at the haven, after much tribulation.

Thursday 30th April

We had lovely weather for May's funeral at 1pm. Finlay Beaton took the prayer meeting for me.

Thursday 7th May

Beauly prayer meeting. Over twenty attended. Rev. D.A. Macfarlane took part of Ezekiel 36:25–26. He said that all who are saved are interested in these promises, although primarily given to the Jews in captivity. All who are interested in these promises are ashamed of themselves for their unholiness and turn all this into prayer. The Lord can change the child in the womb. They come to love hearing about Jesus. The Lord can give you a new heart. Ezekiel had an interest in these three promises, so had Daniel and his fellows.

Friday 8th May

I visited Archie Robertson. He told me he was greatly troubled with the sins and errors of his youth, when he was given to music and playing the bagpipes. He could hardly shake off thinking of these days. However, any discerning person can see that he is a saint of God and approaching the better country.

Tuesday 19th May

In Glasgow for the Synod. I am lodging with Alasdair Gillies, Bentinck Street, with Rev. R.R. Sinclair, Ian Mackenzie, Rev. D.B. MacLeod and the two Tallach students.[340]

Friday 22nd May

Synod ended at 10pm last night. This morning I visited Tommy Macrae at Dennistoun. I never saw one more entertaining—telling edifying stories of bygone days relative to the church and the people of God.

---

[340] Ian R. Tallach (1936–1979), who became minister of the Perth, Stirling and Dundee charge in 1973, and his first cousin John Tallach (son of Rev. James A. Tallach). John Tallach was inducted to the Kinlochbervie and Scourie charge later that year, after which he pastored the Aberdeen FP congregation from 1979 until 1989 when he joined the APC; he later became a minister in the Church of Scotland.

Thursday 28th May

Rev. Aaron Ndebele[341] took a meeting in Dingwall: about sixty attended. He took Revelation 3:8. 'I have set before thee an open door.' All engaged in God's service must be cautious how they go about it: the Lord follows every step.

Sabbath 31st May

Dingwall 6.30pm. Rev. D.A. Macfarlane kindly took my place in Beauly to let me go to hear Aaron Ndebele, who preached from John 20:20.[342] The disciples were in fear of what might befall them when Christ was taken away. The world was glad when Christ was removed. The disciples mourned, and the devil thought he had won the day.

Wednesday 10th June

Left for Shieldaig communion. Rev. Alex MacAskill took the prayer meeting at 7pm, preaching on Psalm 28. He observed three matters:

1. David is brought before us as a man of prayer, which is no small matter and belongs to God's children.

2. The spirit of gratitude given.

3. The enlargement of heart given. This is not in us by nature, we are bound up with ourselves. Where grace is, it will persevere.

Thursday 11th June

Shieldaig communion. At noon, Rev. Alex McPherson said that those who are not exercised in the two graces of

---

[341] Rev. Aaron Ndebele (1925–2004) was minister of the Ingwenya charge in Zimbabwe for 35 years. 'Rev. A.B. Ndebele', *FPM* Vol. 110 (March 2005): pp. 79–85.

[342] 'And when he had so said, he shewed unto them his hands and his side. Then were the disciples glad, when they saw the Lord.'

repentance and faith have not a spark of true religion. He said these two graces are the foundation of growth in grace and the foundation of all profitable remembrance of the Lord's death. There is no more sweet experience than genuine repentance and faith in Christ.

At 6pm Mr MacAskill took Lamentations 5:21. 'Turn thou us unto thee, O Lord, and we shall be turned.' There is no cure for our troubles but in turning to God. His points were:

1. The request to be turned.

2. The confidence the church had that she would be turned.

3. The ground of her confidence, 'Thou, O Lord, remainest for ever; thy throne from generation to generation' (v. 19).

Friday 12th June

Shieldaig communion. Alick Maclennan[343] (Diabeg) gave out the Question from 1 John 2:21.[344] I never heard it taken as the Question before. He wanted marks of those who know the truth. The Question was opened by Mr MacAskill who said, 'I am afraid myself of the epistles of John. They are so spiritual.' Seven spoke.

Sabbath 14th June

Shieldaig communion. At noon Mr MacAskill preached in the Song of Solomon 2:1. 'I am the rose of Sharon, and the lily of the valleys.'

---

[343] Alexander Maclennan (1917–1984) was brother-in-law to Raasay elder Ronald Macbeth and to Rev. Archibald Beaton, Gairloch. 'The late Mr Alexander MacLennan, Elder, Shieldaig', FPM Vol. 90 (May 1985): pp. 154–155.

[344] 'I have not written unto you because ye know not the truth, but because ye know it, and that no lie is of the truth.'

Monday 15th June

Shieldaig communion ends. Rev. McPherson took Revelation 5:9–10 and said, 'You will not get to heaven if you have not learned to sing this song on earth.'

Mr MacAskill and I went to Kenmore to visit John MacCuish, who is becoming very frail.[345] We were in all the houses, arriving in Shieldaig about 10pm.

Tuesday 16th June

Alick Maclennan and I went as far as the Loch Torridon entrance after lunch. We took the long lines but did not feel a bite, the weather being clear. So, we hoisted the sail and came to the anchorage at the Corran about 3pm. It was a lovely outing anyway.

Wednesday 17th June

Lochcarron communion. Mr MacAskill took the prayer meeting in Psalm 28. All who are given grace to pray will not stop because of God's silence—see, for example, Bartimaeus. Where grace is, it will persevere. Where are you to go if you turn from the Lord?

Friday 26th June

Inverness communion. The Question was given out by Neil Ross in Psalm 116:1–2,[346] looking for marks of those who love the Lord.

---

[345] Mr MacCuish (1894–1975) was originally from Harris but had obtained a croft in Kenmore on the south shore of Loch Torridon. 'John MacCuish, Elder, Kenmore', *FPM* Vol. 81 (June 1976): pp. 218–220.

[346] 'I love the Lord, because he hath heard my voice and my supplications. Because he hath inclined his ear unto me, therefore will I call upon him as long as I live.'

Sabbath 28th June

Inverness communion. At 6.30pm Rev. Alex Morrison (Uist) took Daniel 5:30.[347] His first point was how the night was spent—making carnal use of holy things, and making mockery of religion. There was excessive drinking which is ruinous to body and soul, and they were also sinning against light. His second point was how the night ended—it shall be ill with the wicked.

Thursday 2nd July

Beauly communion. Rev. Donald Nicolson preached in Gaelic in Hosea 2:14. 'Therefore, behold, I will allure her, and bring her into the wilderness, and speak comfortably unto her.' God can change men to run towards good, as they once ran towards evil, like Saul of Tarsus. The fire of tribulations will cut the cords that bind his people to the world and the flesh. The church of God will go through fire and water when drawn by the Father. It is through the wilderness that we must go to heaven. Many would go to heaven if they could avoid the wilderness, but this is the school in which God teaches his people.

Rev. Calum MacInnes preached in English from Romans 3:23. 'For all have sinned, and come short of the glory of God.'

Friday 3rd July

Beauly communion. The Question was given out by John Maclennan in Philippians 1:6. 'Being confident of this very thing, that he which hath begun a good work in you will perform it until the day of Jesus Christ.' I referred to being on the west coast in May. It was snowing hard, but the cuckoo was

---

[347] 'In that night was Belshazzar the king of the Chaldeans slain.'

calling vigorously in the birch wood. It was putting me to shame for being so tardy in going to the throne of grace, through lack of spirituality and coldness.

Monday 6ᵗʰ July

Beauly communion ends. In English Rev. Donald Nicolson took Hebrews 11:24.[348] Only God knows when the last trumpet will sound. Pray against this solemn hour. Your time may be drawing near its end. The rich man had great plans when suddenly summoned. Who can understand the wrath of God? 'The wicked shall be turned into hell.' (Psalm 9:17). We are commanded to come to the finished work of Christ. Moses made his choice by faith. The choice you make will determine your fate for ever. If you don't repent you will perish. Moses had everything in abundance, yet he made that particular choice. He knew what he was doing. What are all riches compared to Christ? We should honour the Son as we honour the Father. If we were to give our lives to Christ, we would be the gainers. It is a great matter for any to be called to suffer for Christ. Moses had a reward. All things were included in it. How solemn to think that you are approaching the place where God is seen as He is. It was never more difficult to serve God than now. We are in the beginning of sorrows. God is going to bring this generation through trials.

Friday 17ᵗʰ July

Daviot communion. The Question was given out by Jimmy Macpherson in Psalm 107:14. 'He brought them out of darkness and the shadow of death, and brake their bands in sunder.' Those who spoke were Finlay Beaton, myself, John

---

[348] 'By faith Moses, when he was come to years, refused to be called the son of Pharaoh's daughter.'

Gunn, Mr Mills (London), Captain Roderick Mackay (Harris)[349] and Alex Macpherson. After the evening service, William MacQueen[350] told me that a phone message came saying that John had fainted in the graveyard at Alex Macrae's funeral and had to be taken home. I was alarmed, only having that scanty information. However, we found him on his feet when we called.

Thursday 23rd July

After the prayer meeting we went to John's house. He is slowly improving after the fainting turn he took in Kilmorack cemetery last Friday. He took worship and read two chapters in Thessalonians.

Sabbath 26th July

In Beauly at noon I took 1 Thessalonians 3:11–12 about the Lord directing their hearts into the love of God. My points were:

1. The heart needs to be inclined.
2. There is a twofold aspect to the love of God—his love to us from eternity and the believer's love to him. Profitable subjects for meditation.
3. The patient waiting for Christ.

In Dingwall at 6.30pm I took Psalm 34:6. 'This poor man cried.' Rev. Macfarlane prayed at the close. There was a fairly large congregation.

---

[349] This is most likely to be Roderick Mackay who was an elder in Ness but sailed out of Harris.

[350] Mr MacQueen was a native of Tomatin. 'Tribute to the Late Mr William MacQueen, Elder', *Synod Proceedings May 2001* (Glasgow, 2001): p. 13.

Thursday 30th July

Dingwall communion. At Beauly at 7pm Rev. John MacLeod (Stornoway) preached in Hosea 11:8. 'How shall I give thee up, Ephraim?' He preached a faithful service all through and declared the whole counsel of God.

Friday 31st July

Dingwall communion. I gave out the Question in Psalm 38:4. 'Mine iniquities are gone over my head, as an heavy burden they are too heavy for me.' It was opened by Rev. John MacLeod who said that David learnt his lost condition from the teaching of Heaven. Those speaking were Finlay Beaton, Tom Macrae, John Mackenzie (in Gaelic), Roddy MacDonald (Barlinnie), Angus MacLeod, Willie Sim, Donald Morrison and several others. There were four or five more on the list, but as we were about three hours in, they were not called.

Sabbath 2nd August

Dingwall communion. In Beauly at 6.30pm Rev. Alex Murray (Applecross) took Daniel 5:27.[351] He said that the examination of Belshazzar was final—he was found wanting. The balances are impartial.

Monday 3rd August

Dingwall communion ends. In Gaelic, Rev. John MacLeod took the topic of following Christ, from John 12:26.[352] He said that we haven't enough time to follow vanity and lies

---

[351] 'TEKEL; Thou art weighed in the balances, and art found wanting.'
[352] 'If any man serve me, let him follow me; and where I am, there shall also my servant be: if any man serve me, him will my Father honour.'

but must follow him according to the rules of his Word in humility and dependence.

Friday 7th August

Stratherrick communion. The Question was given out by Ewen Fraser[353] in 1 Peter 2:7.[354] Finlay Beaton said, 'Everything becomes new.' They are strangers on the earth, born from above. They love the Scriptures. They feel their need of the Word of God. They often get nothing from it. They chew the cud. They are lowly in mind. We are dwarves in our day but it is good to be a living dwarf itself.

Monday 10th August

Willie Macrae, Lower Farley, died this evening. He dropped dead sawing sticks. He had taken dinner and afternoon tea as usual. He was about eighty-seven.

Friday 14th August

Bonar Bridge communion. The Question was given out by Donald Campbell in Romans 5:19.[355] Marks were wanted of those who were 'made righteous by the obedient one'. Those

---

[353] Ewen Fraser (1926–2010) was a farmer and elder who often held services. He and his wife Ella lived in Gorthleck. 'Tribute to the late Mr Ewen Fraser', *Synod Proceedings, May 2011* (Glasgow, 2011), pp. 22–24.

[354] 'Unto you therefore which believe he is precious: but unto them which be disobedient, the stone which the builders disallowed, the same is made the head of the corner.'

[355] 'For as by one man's disobedience many were made sinners, so by the obedience of one shall many be made righteous.'

who spoke were myself, Willie Sim, J.A. Davidson, D. Maclennan and Hugh Lobban.[356]

Sabbath 23rd August

I went out feeling very unfit spiritually but the Master sustained me. I enlarged on what I had taken last Thursday—'But my God shall supply all your need according to his riches in glory by Christ Jesus' in Philippians 4:19.

Thursday 27th August

Beauly prayer meeting. About twenty-five attended. I took Psalm 130, from which I observed that all true believers find an echo in their hearts, agreeing to the experience of the Psalmist.

1. The depths mentioned—all believers who have had the least conviction have gone so deep as to know that only Christ can save them. Also they cry to God from the depths of their souls—not half-heartedly but in real earnest.

2. They know they would have no standing if God would 'mark iniquity'. They believe there is forgiveness in God.

3. They are a waiting people, waiting on God and for God.

4. Their hope is in God's Word.

5. They believe that God will keep his promises, just as they believe the morning light will come in its appointed time. The word 'Israel' may suggest that the Psalm can be applied to all who keep wrestling at the throne of grace.

---

[356] An elder in Bonar Bridge, known for his familiarity with the writings of the Puritan John Owen, Mr Lobban later moved to Inverness.

Thursday 3rd September

Ullapool communion. At 6pm Rev. Alfred MacDonald preached from 1 John 1:9. 'If we confess our sins, he is faithful and just to forgive us our sins, and to cleanse us from all un-righteousness.' You may say, 'I will not confess, because I fear judgment.' God asks you to confess your sin with a view to pardon you, but you will not believe it.

Friday 4th September

Ullapool communion. Hector Campbell gave out the Question in Ephesians 2:1.[357] Nine spoke, some were not called. Tom Macrae quoted Rev. Neil Cameron: 'If you went through effectual calling, you can be sure you are elected.' Marks of grace—Christ, his Word, the means of grace and the blood of Christ are precious to them.

Monday 14th September

On the way home from the Inverness prayer meeting we called at a tinker's house. The woman's husband was killed on Saturday night. There were about twenty people present. I went in and prayed, for which they expressed their appreciation.

Tuesday 15th September

I visited John Livingstone at Braefoot. He said he remembered Rev. D.A. Macfarlane giving an exhortation to the people after the tables were served at a communion. Mr Macfarlane said, 'May you have with the Psalmist the words "How sweet unto my taste, O Lord, / are all thy words of

---

[357] 'And you hath he quickened, who were dead in trespasses and sins.'

truth; / yea I do find them sweeter far / than honey to my mouth.'"[358]

Monday 21st September

My wife and I went to Inverness in the afternoon. I called on Finlay Beaton, to ask if he would to go with us to Lochcarron next week. The answer was 'Yes' without a hitch. I admired his pluck and spiritual liveliness in his eighty-seventh year.

Wednesday 23rd September

At Ferintosh. My wife and I were at Rev. Cartwright's manse[359] for tea. If you should ask why I was in a Free Church manse, I would answer, 'Because I take him to be a man of God and I felt I could ask Christ to accompany us, I felt there was no danger of me having to stifle my conscience, I felt I was doing nothing contrary to the example of Christ, and my intention in going was to join in reading the Word of God and prayer.'

Friday 25th September

Donald Campbell, the Free Church missionary in Beauly, called on us. He informed us that it was intended to play football on Sabbath the 27th September. Mr Campbell requested

---

[358] Psalm 119:103, metrical version.

[359] Rev. Hugh M. Cartwright (1943–2011) pastored Ferintosh Free Church from 1969 until 1990, then taught Church History and Church Principles as a professor in the Free Church College in Edinburgh. He joined the FP Church in 1998. In that year he was inducted to Edinburgh FP congregation and remained its minister until his death. He tutored FP divinity students in Greek and New Testament during the Edinburgh pastorate. *Reformation Press* published a collection of his sermons, *With an Everlasting Love* (2015), and it is intended to print further works.

me to write a letter to Lord Lovat[360] to ask if he could intervene in the matter. I endeavoured (in dependence on God) to do this and both of us signed it.

Wednesday 7th October

Left for Gairloch. We stopped at Laide for the prayer meeting. I took John 6:53. 'Except ye eat the flesh of the Son of man, and drink his blood, ye have no life in you.' There would be about seventeen people present; some could not attend.

Monday 12th October

At Gairloch. We had a prayer meeting at 7.30pm. Tommy MacLeod[361] presided. Those praying were Rev. Alfred MacDonald, myself, Sandy, Hector and Willie Sim. Afterwards we went to the Urquhart sisters for worship.

Thursday 15th October

Day of Prayer. Rev. D.A. Macfarlane took John 12:32. 'And I, if I be lifted up from the earth, will draw all men unto me.' He said, 'It is a solemn and terrifying matter to think of men in pulpits in churches with fine organs, going to the flames of hell.' I have my idols and the self-pleasing spirit. He said that one effect of Christ's being lifted up would be to draw men off from the covenant of works. He said how sad it

---

[360] Simon Christopher Joseph Fraser (1911–1995), 15th Lord Lovat and 4th Baron Lovat, was a local landowner and for forty years a member of Inverness County Council. He was known for distinguished war service in Norway and France, and later as a cattle expert.

[361] Tommy Macleod (1896–1981) was a Gairloch elder known for his discernment, love of peace, and humility. 'Mr Thomas Macleod, Elder, Gairloch congregation', FPM Vol. 86 (December 1981): pp. 380–383.

was for mannerly and educated men to be showing they have the spirit of hell before they go into it.

Thursday 22nd October

About twenty people attended the prayer meeting. I took the account of Jesus sending two of his disciples for a colt in Matthew 21:6–7.[362] I noted that the narrative may lead us to make a spiritual use of it. Who does the ass represent? It represents all in the unregenerate state. Who are the two sent to loose it? The Word and the Spirit, or the law and the gospel, or the Old and New Testaments. All must pass Sinai and Calvary on the way to heaven. The ass was tied; so are unregenerate men until loosed. Such a person must be set free by Christ's command before he can move, like Lazarus when loosed from the bonds of death.

Wednesday 28th October

Raasay. Roderick MacLeod and I went visiting at Oighre.[363]

We had the prayer meeting at 7pm. There would be about sixty people at the meeting. Rev. Donald Nicolson preached from John 1:11–13.[364] He said that we see the divinity and eternity of Christ here. All things are upheld by him. He was sustaining the hands of those who were crucifying him. He said that the eye of God is terrible: 'See that it does not look

---

[362] 'And the disciples went, and did as Jesus commanded them, and brought the ass, and the colt, and put on them their clothes, and they set him thereon.'

[363] Eyre, at the southern end of Raasay.

[364] 'He came unto his own, and his own received him not. But as many as received him, to them gave he power to become the sons of God, even to them that believe on his name: which were born, not of blood, nor of the will of the flesh, nor of the will of man, but of God.'

on you, out of Christ. You will never let the world go without the work of the Spirit. You will be miserable for ever if separated from Christ.'

Thursday 29th October

Raasay communion. Rev. Nicolson took Hosea 14:1–3.[365] He said, 'In midst of prosperity you are under the wrath of God, if you are without Christ. You must get words from the Holy Spirit before you can speak to God as you should.'

I visited several homes before going to my lodgings. I received a very warm reception from them all, some of whom were companions from my childhood days.

Friday 30th October

Raasay communion. The Question was given out by John Malcolm[366] in 1 Peter 2:10. 'Which in time past were not a people, but are now the people of God.' About six men spoke to it. Donald Mackay said that this people were once as light as the birds, but they came to see that none could help but Christ. Their daily request is 'God be merciful to me a sinner.' Like the leper they say, 'If thou wilt, thou canst make me clean.' They feel their sins growing heavier. They can do nothing without Christ.

---

[365] 'O Israel, return unto the Lord thy God; for thou hast fallen by thine iniquity. Take with you words, and turn to the Lord: say unto him, Take away all iniquity, and receive us graciously: so will we render the calves of our lips. Asshur shall not save us; we will not ride upon horses: neither will we say any more to the work of our hands, Ye are our gods: for in thee the fatherless findeth mercy.'

[366] John Malcolm Macleod (1904–1996) was from Rona, spent many years in Glasgow and then returned to Raasay where he became an elder in 1969. 'Tribute to Mr John Malcolm Macleod, Elder, Raasay', *Synod Proceedings, May 1997* (Glasgow, 1997), p. 15.

At 6.30pm Mr MacDonald (Gairloch) took Psalm 86:5.[367]

Thursday 12th November

Harvest Thanksgiving Day, Kilmorack. Rev. William Grant took the service as our minister was not well. He took Psalm 105:1–2.[368] The service took about an hour.

Friday 13th November

Tain communion. Question meeting. Donald Maclennan gave out the Question in Philippians 3:3. 'For we are the circumcision, which worship God in the spirit, and rejoice in Christ Jesus, and have no confidence in the flesh.' Those called were Willie Sim, A. Maclennan, D. Campbell, J. Martin and Ian Mackenzie. One of them said, 'If you only go by your feelings, you won't get far. Christ alone should be your foundation.'

Thursday 19th November

Beauly prayer meeting. About twenty attended. John was out tonight. He is slowly picking up.

Saturday 28th November

This is Term Day. It was once common to see carts and lorries passing, laden with furniture, and people going to new homes. I heard of one man who said, 'I am never happier than when setting off for a new home.' I often thought how it should put to shame professing Christians—who claim God is their Father and heaven to be their home—how they shrink at

---

[367] 'For thou, Lord, art good, and ready to forgive; and plenteous in mercy unto all them that call upon thee.'
[368] 'O give thanks unto the Lord; call upon his name: make known his deeds among the people. Sing unto him, sing psalms unto him: talk ye of all his wondrous works.'

the thought of going to it. Death will indeed bring disaster to the wicked.

Monday 30th November

My wife and I were at Inverness this afternoon. We went for tea to the Balmoral, after which we called on Finlay Beaton. He is a wonderful man, ready to talk on any subject.

Sabbath 6th December

At Dingwall I took the 'well of water springing up to everlasting life' in John 4:14. I endeavoured to trace the analogy between water and the grace of God. It is indispensable. Nothing cleanses like it. It is restless until it reaches the ocean. It seeks to the lowest room. It is free to all.

Thursday 10th December

About twenty-two people attended the prayer meeting. I took the man at the pool of Bethesda in John 5. The man waiting for the moving of the water might be taken as an emblem of the poor sinner waiting on the ordinances of the gospel, knowing that the gospel is the only cure for him. He is therefore waiting patiently and prayerfully, will not go away until he gets a cure, and will not take rest until he is assured that his sins are pardoned.

Sabbath 20th December

In Beauly at noon I took John 19:30. 'When Jesus therefore had received the vinegar, he said, It is finished: and he bowed his head, and gave up the ghost.' I observed that we can only wade on the fringes of this ocean. Christ was forsaken of God, which is not true of any other person until they are in hell, from which there is no coming out. I spoke of some of the things which were 'finished'—the sins of his elect, and the ceremonial law.

Monday 28th December

After a visit to a home where the lady of the house fell on the stair a few weeks ago, and got a severe bruising, we went to the Heathmount Hotel for tea. We then went to see Finlay Beaton. I seldom, if ever, saw one of his age with his faculties as alert and clear in his eighty-seventh year. He preached twice yesterday—at Dornoch and Rogart.

Thursday 31st December

About twenty-three attended the prayer meeting. I was led to the words in Psalm 90:12. 'So teach us to number our days, that we may apply our hearts unto wisdom.'

So, the year is at an end. We have every reason to put up our Ebenezer.[369] The future is dark—may we have what the Psalmist rested on: 'This is our God [...]; he will unto death us guide.'[370] It should be a question with me in my eighty-second year if I will see another New Year. If not, may I be willing and cheerful to leave the earth.[371] Good night.

---

[369] 'Then Samuel took a stone, and set it between Mizpeh and Shen, and called the name of it Ebenezer, saying, Hitherto hath the Lord helped us' (1 Samuel 7:12).
[370] Psalm 48:14, an amalgamation of the prose and metrical versions.
[371] Alex died on 1st January 1972.

Notes of addresses

Faith, hope, charity

1 CORINTHIANS 13:13
And now abideth faith, hope, charity, these three;
but the greatest of these is charity.
THURSDAY 20th FEBRUARY 1969
PRAYER MEETING

THE apostle had been speaking largely about gifts in the preceding chapter. 'Covet earnestly the best gifts,' it says in the last verse. Are we not warned against covetousness? Yes! But I was looking at the Gaelic Bible (the Gaelic helps you considerably at times). The Gaelic gives the meaning of 'covet' as 'earnestly desire'. Otherwise, covetousness is a great sin, and a sin of the heart. Well, the apostle had been speaking about gifts and how useless gifts are of themselves. Grace is stronger than gifts. What though a man had gifts? If he does not use them aright they are harmful. An elder in Dingwall once said, 'I am thankful to the Lord I never had gifts for I am afraid of self.'

So, if a man is merely full of knowledge or languages or eloquence, it a great sin and people will not get good from it. A discerning godly person will know the difference between gifts and grace. But there may be gifts without grace and grace without much gifts at all. All of God's people do not have eloquence. The man whose speaking was used in Spurgeon's conversion could do little more than repeat the text, but Spurgeon got good for eternity from it. Now, while we would not belittle gifts, we say that if a man becomes elated and puffed up, they are no use to him. Where gifts are combined with humility and love they are beautiful.

But the last verse of the chapter says, 'And now abideth, faith, hope, charity, these three; but the greatest of these is charity.' This is what will decide our fate forever. Have we got charity? That is, genuine love to God? If you have that, it will always carry you through, although you may have very few gifts.

Faith

'Now abideth faith.' All God's people have faith. We cannot be justified by works, and although we hear this, we must learn of it by experience, that by the deeds of the law there is no salvation. The people of God are convinced that there is no salvation by the works of the law, and as Paul when tossed up and down on the Sea of Adria said, 'All hope that we should be saved was taken away.' Well, I believe God's people can say that all hope of being saved by the works of the law was taken away from them. And if that is the case, you are ready for union with Christ.

We must be emptied, turned upside down and indebted to Christ alone for salvation. Jonah was in such a situation, that he did not expect anything but death, when he came to this, that 'salvation is of the Lord'. Jonah was not ready for being vomited onto dry land. The Catechism question gives a very comprehensive answer to what saving faith is: 'Faith in Jesus Christ is a saving grace, whereby we receive and rest upon him alone for salvation, as he is offered to us in the gospel.'[372] But though faith is that which saves you, alas, you cannot believe! God must enable you. You must not be discouraged. God will enable you to be saved in a saving manner. It is simple and difficult.

Have you the witness of your conscience that you believe the record God gives of his Son in Matthew, Mark, Luke, John? God's people can say, 'I believe that record, if I believe anything. And I build any hope for eternity on it.' Well, you have saving faith if you can say this. What is the proof that you have saving faith? It will be seen in works that will accompany it. You will do all in your power towards working out your salvation: reading the Holy Scriptures, secret prayer, and attending the ordinances. But the late Rev. Neil Cameron, Glasgow, was saying about this faith, 'Many of God's people cannot say that they are dead sure of salvation, but they could give their oath that God can save them and that he has the power to forgive sin on earth. And they pray to him, and such are safe.'

'The blood of Jesus cleanses from all sin.' The man who believes that—that is faith that is God-given. So the man that has the witness in himself—the witness of his conscience that he honours all the means of God's appointment—he has saving faith. Although you cannot believe, when God will enable you, you will do. 'Lord,' said another, 'I believe; help thou mine unbelief.' And is not faith accompanied by doubts and fears? Yes, frequently. But why doubts and fears? I would say that anything that keeps you on your two knees will not be in vain. Well, it may serve that purpose—to keep his people on their knees, meek and humble, and not presumptuous but waiting on their Lord.

---

[372] *Shorter Catechism*, answer 86.

Hope

Faith is first, then hope. You must not make a saviour of your faith. You may make an idol of your faith instead of looking to the object of faith—Jesus Christ. 'Faith is the hand that grasps.'

Well, even one of the poets has said, 'Hope springs eternal from the human breast.'[373] There is nothing to be compared to hope. What is the difference between a good hope and a false hope? Well, the good hope has Scriptural foundations. It is from the Word. You take your support if you hope because Christ has died for your sins, if you hope because Christ worked out a righteousness for you and because his Spirit can sanctify you and make you fit for heaven. That hope will never put you to shame.

There are others who hope because they have heard many great sermons and know great and godly men. Well, though a man would live like an angel, it would be a poor foundation going to eternity. Those who have a good hope, hope in God's mercy. There is in effectual calling an apprehension of the mercy of God in Christ, and that puts a man to pray. He has a secret apprehension that God has mercy in store for him and that encourages him to pray and to keep on praying. Dr Kennedy said, 'Hope is better than assurance.' The way I was working that out is: assurance may leave you, but a good hope remains. And one of the Puritans says, 'Assurance is a pearl which the Lord will not allow his people near but on special occasions.'

---

[373] *An Essay on Man* by Alexander Pope (1688–1744).

Charity

'And charity'—or the Scripture sense of it—love. 'They shall have their dwelling there that love his blessed name.'[374] Love is the most pleasant passion of the human soul. What is more easy than to love, and the soul that can say he feels love to God and to all that is his, has cause to believe that God loved him first. One of the Puritans said, 'A man may not be able to say much about conversion, but ask him what things he loves. He can say, "I love the preaching of the Gospel. I love the Word of God and the people of God."'

A man is not at a loss to know what he loves. So, if you find marks of that love which is a desire to please God, it is a good mark on you.

There is a desire for union where there is genuine love. Well, you desire union with Christ above everything else. It is said that lovers love to be alone. And where there is a desire for secret communion with God in secret prayer, it is the best sign of genuine love. Many can speak to the dog and to the cat but have no intercourse between them and heaven. If there is a state of war between two countries, you won't see the ships of the enemy in the ports of the other enemy. If there is no intercourse with heaven, it is to be feared there is a state of war between you and God.

We should never rest until we bear marks of genuine love to God. The Day of Judgment need not be a cause of fear if you love his appearance. When others will call on the rocks and hills to cover them, you have nothing to fear. You will have a friend at court. You know the Gaelic saying: 'A friend

---

[374] Adaptation of Psalm 69:36, metrical version: 'And they that are his servants' seed / inherit shall the same; / so shall they have their dwelling there / that love his blessed name.'

at court is better than five shillings in the purse.' Christ will be your friend if you love him in sincerity and truth.

New Year's Day service 1970

PSALM 100

Make a joyful noise unto the Lord, all ye lands. Serve the Lord with gladness: come before his presence with singing. Know ye that the Lord he is God: it is he that hath made us, and not we ourselves; we are his people, and the sheep of his pasture. Enter into his gates with thanksgiving, and into his courts with praise: be thankful unto him, and bless his name. For the Lord is good; his mercy is everlasting; and his truth endureth to all generations.

THURSDAY 1ˢᵗ JANUARY 1970

THIS is a psalm of praise which calls upon all people to praise the Lord. There are many songs sung at this time of year, not to the praise of God.

There is reference here to the noise of the jubilee trumpet. Notice it was a joyful sound. This noise was music to the slave. And we ourselves are slaves in a spiritual sense. 'Whosoever committeth sin is the servant of sin' [John 8:34]. We serve the devil and that is slavery indeed. We have lost our righteousness. All that is worth having now is the favour of God.

We are told to make a joyful noise with reason. Liberty is proclaimed to the captives of sin and Satan. What fearful bondage unregenerate sinners are in, spending their lives worshipping creatures!

The new creature has a new song. They sing with a new heart. 'A new heart also will I give you' [Ezekiel 36:26]. God himself promises to give this to you. Who ever heard the like?

A new creation. How do I know if I have this? You may know if you can say that you have had two days.[375] Our affections have been moved heavenwards. You now follow the means of grace. You love the Scriptures. There is much done outwardly by example and by education but that is not sufficient. We cannot have God without a new creation.

It is a song for the new covenant. If we have it, we will have a New Year and get a blessing. If you are under the old covenant, you are growing poorer and poorer every year. Those who are united to Christ are growing in grace.

---

[375] This is a Gaelic-based expression meaning 'you have changed a great deal'.

The crucifixion

MATTHEW 27:37–66
And set up over his head his accusation written, This is Jesus the King of the Jews (etc.)
PRAYER MEETING

1. The title on the cross was written in three languages. There were, we are told, millions in Jerusalem at that time. At the Day of Judgment the sins of sinners will be revealed. You would not like your thoughts of an hour to be written on these walls. Well, there is nothing secret that shall not be made known. I, for my part, am glad that it is written: 'It is the glory of God to conceal a matter' [Proverbs 25:2].

2. The darkness. It is owing to the mercy of God that we have natural light, and that the sun runs its daily course in the heavens. I knew a godly woman who, when she would see the sun shining on her wall on a winter's day, would say, 'What a wonder that the sun shines on a wicked world!' The sun went into mourning for its Creator, and we think that it would not have shone again had Christ not been able to finish the work given him to do.

3. Forsaken. No man in this world is completely forsaken. There are drops of mercy mixed with the sorest of judgments.

It is in hell that men are forsaken by God and by one another. I say these things that you may fall down and seek mercy *now*, otherwise there will be none to comfort you. Christ said, 'I thirst.' Compare what it says of the rich man (Luke 16), that he asked for a drop of water. Yes, even a drop is denied to sinners in hell.

4. The rocks rending and the veil of the temple torn in pieces. Our own hearts are harder than the rocks. The veil rent meant that the way into the Holiest opened, and also that the partition wall between Jew and Gentile was demolished. (Referred to the Berlin Wall).[376]

5. The bodies of the saints rose. We are not told what happened to these, but they would go to heaven in a way consistent with his honour and glory. The opening of the graves signified an assurance of the rising again from spiritual death; also the final resurrection.

6. Joseph. Joseph did not grudge his tomb. It is often in a time of trial that one who has been in the background comes out. He may have thought, 'It will be my own again in three days.'

---

[376] From 1949 to 1989, West Berlin was an enclave controlled by the Allies (UK, USA and France) and then by the former West Germany. In 1961 the Communists built the Berlin Wall to prevent people escaping from their rule in surrounding East Germany. Much of it was three to four metres in height and included guard towers and an adjacent 'death strip'. East German protesters began demolishing the wall on 9th November 1989, marking the first step towards the eventual reunification of Germany.

7. Death of Christ. Rev. D.A. Macfarlane said, 'The one-horned animal used to gore its prey. So Christ gored Satan and destroyed him that has the power of death.'

The woman and the dragon

REVELATION 12:1–3
And there appeared a great wonder in heaven; a woman clothed with the sun, and the moon under her feet, and upon her head a crown of twelve stars: and she being with child cried, travailing in birth, and pained to be delivered. And there appeared another wonder in heaven; and behold a great red dragon, having seven heads and ten horns, and seven crowns upon his heads.

THE Revelation is a difficult book from which to get some benefit, except as God's Spirit will lead.

The woman may signify the Church of God—the Apostolic Church.

Clothed with the sun: Christ is the righteousness of the Church. 'Put ye on the Lord Jesus Christ.' 'As the sun shineth in his strength'—what a glorious emblem!

The moon under her feet. The moon is an emblem of change: hence the world, with its honours, its wealth, often changes hands. The true Church has the world under its feet. May also be a reference to the ceremonial law. These Jews

who were in Christ had the ceremonial law under their feet—
but with great difficulty.

The crown of twelve stars. Twelve refers to the twelve
tribes of Israel and also the twelve apostles of the Lamb, i.e.
not any particular church. The true glory of the Church is the
doctrines of the twelve apostles—the true Church of the body
of believers.

She travailed. When Sion travailed, she brought forth children. The true believer travails for souls.

The dragon. Satan is never far away whenever a good
work is being wrought. (In the sense of 'in the church';
compare with Nehemiah.)

The unjust steward

LUKE 16:1–8

And he said also unto his disciples, There was a cer-
tain rich man, which had a steward; and the same
was accused unto him that he had wasted his goods.
And he called him, and said unto him, How is it that
I hear this of thee? give an account of thy steward-
ship; for thou mayest be no longer steward (etc.).

I BELIEVE this chapter has a connection with verse 13 of
the preceding chapter: 'And not many days after the
younger son gathered all together, and took his journey into a
far country, and there wasted his substance with riotous living.'
The younger son wasted his substance that he had received
from his father—not a good steward of the inheritance he had
been given.

The resourcefulness of the unjust steward is not to be cop-
ied.

A steward had to be an honest man. He is one who stands
between two parties. What he has is not his own. Nothing
that we have is our own—except our sin. God gives us time in
drops—only the present moment is our own. Our lifetime is

not our own. Our money is not our own: every penny in the
bank is God's. We are not the owners. 'The earth is the
Lord's.'

What have we that we have not received? Family, wives,
etc. are not our own. All gifts are from God. So are gospel
privileges. They are God-given: ours for a while only.

The lessons

1. Do not seek to make a nest in this world. The Trini-
tarian Bible [Society] man was telling us on Thursday evening
how pointless it would be for them to procure a new building,
where they well knew that the demolition squad would come
in a few years' time. So, we should not build our nest here
(Rutherford). We cannot call anything our own—my home,
my wife. No! There should be less of this talk.

2. Use our time aright. How many waste their time in the
ungodly conversation of the world, instead of praying! Our
aim should be that every faculty of our soul and every member
of our body should be used in the service of God. But this is
impossible without the new nature—'Except ye be converted
and become as little children' (Matthew 18:3). Every person
who is not in Christ is wasting his time.

3. Use your money aright. If you are more careful about
gathering a little of the dust of this world than you are about
distributing it for the good of the Cause of Christ, that is a sign
that you love the world. 'The love of money is the root of all
evil' (1 Timothy 6:10). Some go to the desert places of the
world where there is no gospel to scrape a little of its gold. A
good guide regarding giving to the Cause of Christ is to give
at least a tenth (tithe) and to add thereto, just as David said to

Solomon, when he himself had prepared for the building of the temple (1 Chronicles 22:14).

4. Use your gospel privileges aright. The time is soon coming when those will be at an end. The gospel trumpet will not sound in the caverns of a lost eternity. Soon we shall be ousted out of our time, money and privileges. Our conscience will accuse us that we have wasted our goods. The conscience of the wicked man is like a sleeping puppy outside a door—no alarm to the householder. So man's conscience allows a man to do any wickedness. But at death it will be awakened and never be quietened. God's law will accuse us. There is 'one that accuses' you, 'even Moses' [John 5:45].

Sinners will remember the good times they had on earth. 'Remember that thou in thy lifetime' etc. The end of all things is at hand. 'Thou mayest be no longer steward.' The wealth of the wicked is laid up for the just. The Jews were stewards and had wasted their goods by putting a gloss on the Scriptures.

Fragments

PSALM 105:1
O give thanks unto the Lord; call upon his name:
make known his deeds among the people.
14ᵀᴴ NOVEMBER 1957, HARVEST THANKSGIVING

1. 'Give thanks.' One can never truly give thanks until one's sins are pardoned. 'Thanks be to God for his unspeakable gift' [2 Corinthians 9:15]. The believer although he would have little of the world—and lose all he has—can say, 'Why complain I do not have the streams when I have the spring— the fountainhead?' Achsah was given the 'upper springs' as well as the 'nether springs'.

The rich man did not have the spirit of thankfulness for what he had in this world, and in hell he did not have even a drop of water. We do not have miracles such as the manna, but we are constantly provided for, all the same.

I saw a man one Thanksgiving Day digging in his garden, and I said to him, 'Why are you not going to church?'

He replied, 'I forgot. But what have I to thank God for anyway, who has only given me this hard patch of earth?' This is the spirit of the world.

2. 'Call on his name.' Not in a formal way. Compare Saul of Tarsus before and after conversion. Once at worship, a man when asked to ask the blessing, said, 'I have not learned the proper phraseology.' It is desire that gives wings to prayer.

3. 'Make known his deeds among the people.' 'To men his deeds make known' [metrical version]. This is a mark of grace—a desire to evangelise. It is those who speak of Christ, to whom he will draw near. Compare the two on the way to Emmaus.

JOSHUA 2:15–17
Then she let them down by a cord through the window: for her house was upon the town wall, and she dwelt upon the wall. And she said unto them, Get you to the mountain, lest the pursuers meet you; and hide yourselves there three days, until the pursuers be returned: and afterward may ye go your way. And the men said unto her, We will be blameless of this thine oath which thou hast made us swear.
SABBATH 23ʳᵈ OCTOBER 1966[377]

My mind recurs to the *Pilgrim's Progress*. After the land of Beulah, the pilgrims rush onward to the celestial city, but they soon come to a river where they see many trials waiting. 'Is there no way across?' No; it is appointed for men once to die. Only Enoch and Elijah did not have to cross. The wicked will be carried down the river of death to the Dead Sea. 'If thou

---

[377] The Sabbath after the death of Robert Watt, an elder in Inverness. See footnote for 25ᵗʰ January 1957.

hast run with the footmen and they have wearied thee, what wilt thou do in the swellings of Jordan?' [Jeremiah 5:12].

JOHN 16:27
For the Father himself loveth you, because ye have loved me, and have believed that I came out from God.
17TH DECEMBER 1970, PRAYER MEETING

Love is the most pleasing of the passions. Pray daily for the living graces of faith and love; this will land you safely on the other side (of death).

PROVERBS 6:6–11
Go to the ant, thou sluggard; consider her ways, and be wise: which having no guide, overseer, or ruler, provideth her meat in the summer, and gathereth her food in the harvest. How long wilt thou sleep, O sluggard? when wilt thou arise out of thy sleep? Yet a little sleep, a little slumber, a little folding of the hands to sleep: so shall thy poverty come as one that travelleth, and thy want as an armed man.
(NO DATE)

What a condition man must be in, when he, the chief of God's creation with extensive powers of intellect etc., is now commanded to go to the ant for instruction! The sluggard may be very active in brain and muscle but spiritually he is so dead: he cannot—will not—take one step God-ward.

The ants—no guide, overseer or ruler, and yet provide meat for their existence.

We have all had, I suppose, spiritual guides from our infancy: godly parents, teachers, ministers, elders. Some, too, had godly relations.

Harvest and summers indicate seasons of prosperity—health, hearing, eyesight. An old missionary in Beauly used to say, 'You don't wait until the roads are blocked with snowdrifts to go to gather in your harvest.'

'One that travelleth.' Such a one is soon at his destination. We are travellers from time to eternity—soon we will be at the end of the journey.

'An armed man'. One cannot do anything when faced with such a man. It's 'Hands up!' then.

MARK 16
The Resurrection.
SABBATH MORNING (NO DATE)

It was fitting that when the natural sun was rising on the earth, the Sun of Righteousness should rise from his grave early in the morning. The morning is a beautiful time—how suited it is for prayer and meditation!

Anecdotes

PSALM 37:1–4
Fret not thyself because of evildoers, neither be thou envious against the workers of iniquity. For they shall soon be cut down like the grass, and wither as the green herb. Trust in the Lord, and do good; so shalt thou dwell in the land, and verily thou shalt be fed. Delight thyself also in the Lord; and he shall give thee the desires of thine heart.

ALEX told the story of a gentleman who was going out to shoot, and who took with him a shepherd who was reputed to have been good at telling what kind of weather to expect.

The gentleman asked the shepherd, 'What weather will it be today?'

'Well,' said the shepherd, 'whatever weather it will be, it will please me *well*.'

'How so?' replied the gentleman.

Said the shepherd, 'Because it will be what it pleases God to send. And what pleaseth God pleaseth me.'

Dr Kennedy was once going up a long drive which led to a titled gentleman's manor, whom he intended to visit along with his coachman. When they were about halfway up the drive they met the gentleman in question along with his wife. After some conversation they parted. Said Dr Kennedy to his coachman, 'What an awful thought came into my mind while we were conversing with the lady and her husband!' He then quoted to his coachman these words: 'How in a moment suddenly, to ruin brought are they.'[378] Soon after this excursion, the lady was found drowned in Lochalsh, and her husband died soon after from an incurable disease.

---

[378] Psalm 73:19, metrical version.

The conversion of Saul of Tarsus

Address on Acts 9
SABBATH 5TH MARCH 1961
STRATHY POINT, SUTHERLAND[379]

PAUL was the brightest star in the New Testament firmament. He scaled heights which ordinary Christians will never attain to. I will however point out to some features in his conversion which every true Christian must experience in more or less degree.

1. He was struck by a divine supernatural light. This is true of every believer—no amount of education, sharpness of brain, example or good moral upbringing will bring him to see the things that belong to his peace—to see Christ as the way to heaven. 'The dayspring from on high' visits them [Luke 1:78].

---

[379] Alex wrote these notes in a letter to Elizabeth dated 7th March 1961, describing it as a 'skeleton' of his 'discourse'. This is the only specimen from his own pen, whereas the other addresses in this book are the notes of hearers.

'O send thy light forth' [Psalm 43:3, metrical version]. 'The people which sat in darkness saw a great light' [Matthew 4:16].

They are convinced they could not find the gate of heaven by any natural light or learning, any more than the Sodomites could find the door of Lot's house (although beside them) when struck with blindness, nor Hagar find the well until it was shown to her. The sun cannot be seen until it reveals itself. Christ must rise upon the soul before he is seen to be God manifest in the flesh—ascribing to him all the attributes of deity, etc.

2. Saul of Tarsus fell to the ground. The believer in Christ came to see he can do nothing. 'They fell, no help could have' [Psalm 107:12, metrical version]. 'For by the works of the law shall no flesh be justified' [Galatians 2:16]. As the Ethiopian cannot change his skin [Jeremiah 13:23] and 'without me ye can do nothing' [John 15:5]. 'Not unto us, Lord, not to us, / but do thou glory take' [Psalm 115:1, metrical version]. He must come to acknowledge that 'salvation is of the Lord' [Jonah 2:9] and that 'not we, but he us made' [Psalm 100:3, metrical version]. 'Not by works of righteousness which we have done, but according to his mercy he saved us' [Titus 3:5]. When the soul sees the extensive compass of the law, he despairs of being able to do anything in matters of justification. Whoever has anything that will stand, he sees he has nothing, no more than Satan.

3. Saul of Tarsus said, 'What wilt thou have me to do?' Those truly converted will desire to know what their duty is. They desire to trample on their own will—pleasure—profit. And they desire that God's will would be done in them and by them. 'Bringing into captivity every thought to the obedience of Christ' [2 Corinthians 10:5]. 'Nevertheless not my will, but

thine, be done' [Luke 22:42]. They search the scriptures to find out the will of God and the terms on which they can have salvation. They accept these terms are well pleased with them—even to renounce all merit in anything they can say or do. They always put the Lord before them—fervently desire that his will be done in them and by them. The promise to them: 'He that doeth the will of God abideth for ever' (1 John 2:4). 'For whosoever shall do the will of God, the same is my brother, and my sister, and mother' [Mark 3:35].

4. Saul of Tarsus began to pray. This is a characteristic of a newborn soul. The spirit of prayer is given to them. No notice is taken of Saul's prayers prior to his meeting with Christ on way to Damascus. After this meeting, the Holy Spirit records of him, 'Behold he prayeth' [Acts 9:11]. Prayer is the breath of the new creature, and the spiritual life in him is in proportion to the degree to which he is exercised in this important duty. Let no one say, 'I'm too busy to attend to it.' Daniel had the affairs of over 180 provinces to superintend and he could find time to open his window three times a day towards Jerusalem. Someone said, 'The man who is too busy to pray is busier than God ever intended him to be.' Prayer is a sign of God's elect. Don't say, 'I cannot pray.' If a divine light has struck you, you will see your needs to be so profound that the only thing you can do is pray about it. You know how it fared with the publican. His prayer did not take up much time. Compare that with the prayer of the destitute. If you don't pray, you will regret it.

5. He, Saul of Tarsus, joined himself to people of God. (This is true in conversion—they seek company of people of God). We think this is a sure mark of those who will be in heaven. They love the company of the spiritually minded.

Their conversation is on heavenly things when they meet with those who can engage in it. 'I am companion to all those / who fear, and thee obey' [Psalm 119:63, metrical version]. 'We know that we have passed from death unto life, because we love the brethren' [1 John 3:14]. There is no company the new creation will feel as comfortable with, or so much at home with, as the people of God. Saul was at one time an enemy to them. His attitude towards them changed from the day Christ met with him on way to Damascus. Saul needed no more letters from the High Priest to drag people of God to prison after Christ met him.

The truly converted will seek the welfare of God's people, regard them as the salt of the earth and the lights of the world, honour them, and regard it as a privilege to be with them, to have contact with them. They regard any place a wilderness if none of God's people are there. 'What have I here, saith the Lord, that my people is taken away for nought?' [Isaiah 52:5].

6. Saul separated from his old companions. Those converted to God will invariably forsake their sinful companions. They cannot mix with the world. Though there was only a paling between them and the ungodly, they cannot mix with them. Their language is from the day Christ met them, 'All ye that evil-doers are / from me depart away' [Psalm 119:115, metrical version]. 'What have I to do any more with idols?' [Hosea 14:8]. 'For the time past of our life may suffice us to have wrought the will of the Gentiles, when we walked in lasciviousness, lusts, excess of wine, revellings, banquetings, and abominable idolatries' [1 Peter 4:3]. They lose their relish for the companions of unregenerate days. They are now resolved to cast in their lot with people of God. Can you put your feet in their steps?

Printed in Poland
by Amazon Fulfillment
Poland Sp. z o.o., Wrocław